PRACTICE WITH
IDIOMS

PRACTICE WITH
IDIOMS

Ronald E. Feare

American Language Institute
San Diego State University

OXFORD UNIVERSITY PRESS

Oxford University Press

200 Madison Avenue
New York, N.Y. 10016   USA

Walton Street
Oxford OX2 6DP   England

OXFORD is a trademark of Oxford University Press.

ISBN 0-19-502782-5

Printing (last digit): 19 18 17 16 15 14 13 12

Printed in the United States of America.

Contents

man-to-man, narrow-minded, first-rate, stuck-up,
close-mouthed)

APPENDIX

INDEX

Preface

The purpose of this workbook is to encourage the active participation of the learner in acquiring knowledge of the meaning and structure of American idiomatic expressions. It is believed that students of English, especially those of the intermediate and advanced levels at which this book is aimed, are capable of searching for and discovering much of the relevant information regarding proper idiom usage with only minimal guidance and instruction from the teacher. This active involvement in the learning process can be of much greater benefit to the student than simple memorization.

To achieve this goal, the author has chosen to employ inductive, problem-solving techniques in this workbook which focus on the meaning and structure of American idiomatic expressions. Much emphasis has been placed on the ability to guess meaning from the context within which an idiom is used, and on the ability to figure out the grammatical features which distinguish certain sets of idioms. Once students are equipped with the necessary skills for analyzing and understanding idiomatic forms, they will be in a much better position to expand their knowledge beyond the scope of this workbook.

Few idiom textbooks currently available address themselves in any systematic way to the definable characteristics of idiomatic expressions. As a result, students learning English as a Second or Foreign Language often come to believe that idioms are insurmountable obstacles standing in the way of fluent control of the language. This attitude is particularly distressing because idioms play such an important role in all aspects of communication; without command of idiomatic expressions, students cannot truly feel comfortable and confident in their efforts to master English thoroughly.

It is hoped that the new approach incorporated in this workbook will serve to alleviate many of the difficulties encountered by students in their study of American idioms, and by instructors in their efforts to teach them.

Acknowledgments

I would like to thank Dr. Ann Johns of the American Language Institute, San Diego State University, for her encouragement and advice in the preparation of this workbook, and Dr. Suzette Elgin, Department of Linguistics, San Diego State University, for her many useful suggestions for improving the organization and format of this text.

I would further like to acknowledge A. P. Cowie and R. Mackin whose text, *Oxford Dictionary of Current Idiomatic English*, proved valuable in confirming the presentation of the grammatical categories used in this book.

To the Instructor

HOW TO USE THIS BOOK

Practice With Idioms is a workbook designed for intermediate and advanced level students of English as a Second or Foreign Language who have a basic knowledge of grammatical terms. The book may be effectively used at the high school, college, and university levels, as well as in adult education and intensive language center programs.

The workbook format of *Practice With Idioms* encourages the student to guess the meaning of idiomatic expressions by using contextual information. Use of this workbook requires some basic awareness of English grammar. Such terms as "subject," "verb," "preposition," and "transitive/intransitive" should be well understood before an instructor attempts to use this book. The author would strongly suggest that the instructor preview chapters before work with the students begins, especially those units which deal with the important grammatical characteristics. In addition, it is suggested that the instructor preview the **Appendix,** which provides an explanation of the grammatical terms used in this book and which serves as a handy reference outline of all the grammatical structures. The **Appendix** should prove very useful for both student and teacher when talking about the grammar rules.

The instructor should find the exercises to be self-explanatory for the most part and should have little trouble in advising students of the work to be done. The instructor should soon feel comfortable in guiding students through their work, helping them to discover and understand for themselves the rules and concepts associated with the various idiomatic expressions.

ORGANIZATION

Each chapter of this workbook, with the exception of the review chapters, is made up of the same set of exercises. The idioms are divided into chapters according to their grammatical category. The chapters covering intransitive verbal idioms form **Section I** of the book; chapters covering transitive verbal idioms form **Section II.** Chapters covering nominal, adjectival, and adverbial idioms form **Section III,** which is intended primarily as supplementary material for those advanced students who move rapidly through **Sections I** and **II.** It is believed that verbal forms are more useful in general and deserve far greater concentration and effort. This is the reason why they constitute the larger and more important sections of the book.

WORKING THROUGH A CHAPTER

Part I, a guessing exercise which begins each chapter, requires the student to analyze the contextual setting of the idiom and to extract an appropriate definition or synonym. In addition, the student is asked to underline those clues in the sentence which help him to guess the possible meaning of the idiom. These tasks foster and refine the student's ability to rely on his own knowledge and skill in deciding on meaning. This exercise also promotes class discussion and tends to limit student dependence on dictionaries as a source of definition. It is important to realize that there are no "correct" answers at this initial stage; the student is merely trying to provide some possible, acceptable meanings for the idioms. No attention should be given at this point to the grammar of the idioms, as this is covered thoroughly in following parts and would be a premature consideration.

Part II, a matching exercise, provides the student with a way to check the guesses made in **Part I.** The definitions are listed on the left side of sentences which have blanks to be filled in with appropriate idioms; the sentences are comprised of context clues which are very similar to the ones found in **Part I.** The student can take a definition and check the context of the sentence, go back to **Part I** to match up the definition and context with the correct idiom, and then place that idiom in its proper blank. The instructor would guide the student through this process, helping him to notice similar contexts when difficulties arise. In this way the student can develop his ability to discover the meaning himself before resorting to outside references, such as dictionaries.

Part III provides a detailed explanation of each idiom. Information includes a listing of the most common noun phrases which are associated with each idiom. When necessary, further useful points on grammar or meaning are given. Some example sentences show how the common noun phrases are used with the particular idiom. A set of possible discussion topics is also provided to encourage student feedback and the sharing of ideas with each other and with the instructor.

Part IV focuses on the grammatical features which tie the idioms in each chapter together. A brief introduction provides the student with the basic grammatical framework of the chapter. The student is then asked to compare and analyze sets of contrasting sentences, some correct and some incorrect, which draw out the relevant grammatical features. After he has tried to discover the rules by answering the questions posed, the student finds an explanation of the information which he tried to uncover. It is highly recommended that the instructor preview this part before starting each new chapter.

Part V is a multiple-choice test of idiom understanding and retention. Review is cumulative through each of the first two sections of the book, so in later chapters the student must be careful to follow the correct grammar rules as well as pay attention to the important contextual information. In addition to discussing why an answer is correct, it is also useful to discuss the inappropriateness of other choices as a way to differentiate between the various verbal forms.

Part VI requires the student to write a brief, original sentence using an idiom in correct response to a specific question. The context is provided but must be developed appropriately.

All the exercises and parts of each chapter in **Sections I** and **II** build on the idioms from previous chapters, so that idioms already learned are constantly being reviewed. This also applies to **Section III,** although verbal forms are not included as review.

REVIEW

The review chapters for **Sections I** and **II** also provide valuable reinforcement of grammatical forms, as well as useful information about changing the verbal idioms into nominal (noun) and passive (verb) forms. In addition, topics for paragraph writing, role-playing, and further discussion are provided as interesting ways for students to apply the knowledge they have learned.

ALTERNATE FORMS

It is important to note that some of the idioms which are used in this workbook may have other meanings which have not been included. The author has found it confusing for students to try to grasp too many distinct meanings and forms of the same idiom, and thus has avoided this in the workbook. The instructor should keep this fact in mind, but should concentrate primarily on the meanings and forms provided in this text.

TEACHER AS FACILITATOR

Until students begin to feel comfortable with the new approach in this workbook, all exercises should be done in class, preferably as group activities or on an individual-student basis with the instructor moving around the room offering advice. Optimally, the first two chapters would be done entirely as group activities. It is the author's suggestion that the first two exercises in each chapter also be done in class in order to promote discussion and to discourage students from looking ahead to **Part III** to find the answers. Only the last two exercises in each chapter are recommended for outside homework at any stage or level. The instructor should use his or her own discretion in differentiating classwork and homework as he or she becomes familiar with the students' abilities. The instructor will probably be most involved in the third and fourth parts of each chapter, as they delineate the semantic and syntactic features of the idioms and therefore require more explanation.

To the Student

What exactly is an idiom? This is not an easy question to answer, because many parts of speech may be called idioms. In general, however, an idiom is an expression which has a special meaning, and this meaning cannot be understood completely by looking at the individual words in the idiom.

In this workbook, you will be studying the grammar rules of idioms, as well as the meanings. These rules will describe and distinguish various kinds of idioms; if you are able to separate and understand these different types, you will have an easier time using the idioms you have studied as well as learning new ones. Look at the following examples:

1. I **went over** my speech well.
2. The politician's speech **went over** well.

In each sentence, you are looking at an idiom which has its own special meaning. In the first example, **to go over** means "to review"; in the second example, however, it means "to be received (by an audience)." You should also notice that each idiom is described in a different grammatical way. In the first case, **go over** is followed by a noun, and in the second case, **go over** cannot be followed by a noun. This grammatical difference is one of the many you will learn in this book.

This brief introduction should give you an idea of the new material you will be learning in this book, but learning new material is not all that you will be doing. Slowly but surely you will be learning new ways to guess the meaning of unfamiliar idioms by yourself. A student who develops the necessary skills of guessing will be better prepared to learn the new, and more difficult, idioms he or she encounters outside of class.

INTRANSITIVE
VERBAL IDIOMS

1

Intransitive Verbs with Particles

to die down   to get around   to break in
to come about   to fall through   to catch on
to break down   to hold on   to look on
to get ahead   to open up   to settle down
to stand out   to come up   to show up

I. GUESSING THE MEANING FROM CONTEXT

You can learn a lot about an idiom if you look at the *context* of its use. The meaning of the words around it, and the meaning of the whole sentence, can give you a good idea of the idiom's meaning. You don't need a dictionary to understand the *general meaning* of the idiom.

Try to guess the meaning of each idiom as it is used in the following sentences. Provide either a one-word synonym or a definition.

1. For three days the wind blew hard and strong, but on the fourth day it **died down.**   _____

2. I thought John and Mary were happy, but they recently got a divorce; how did it **come about?**   _____

3. My old car has a very bad engine; it will probably **break down** and need repairs.   _____

4. If you want to **get ahead** in life, you have to work hard and save your money.   _____

5. His poor clothes really **stood out** at the meeting because everyone else was wearing a suit and tie.   _____

6. Since you don't have a car or motorcycle, how do you **get around?**   _____

7. Our plans for a trip to Europe **fell through** because we hadn't saved enough money for the plane tickets. _____

8. Please **hold on;** I'd like to ask a question before you continue your lecture. _____

9. He told me all of his marriage problems, from beginning to end; he really **opened up.** _____

10. Because several students didn't understand the teacher's ideas, many questions **came up.** _____

11. While I was talking, Tom **broke in** to tell me that he disagreed. _____

12. After I spent two hours trying to explain the difficult idea, John finally **caught on.** _____

13. While his friends were playing football, poor Joe, who had a broken leg, could only **look on.** _____

14. At first the students in my class were too noisy, but eventually they **settled down** to work. _____

15. It's already 10 o'clock and Bill hasn't come yet; if he doesn't **show up** soon, our meeting will fall through. _____

Now go back to each sentence in this exercise and <u>underline</u> any part of the sentence which helped you to guess the meaning of the idiom. In other words, try to find the *context clues.*

Class discussion:

You probably could guess the meaning of some idioms more easily than others. Decide which idioms were easy to guess and which were difficult. Discuss the importance of context clues in helping you understand the meaning of each idiom.

II. DEFINITION CORRESPONDENCE

Using **Exercise I** to help you, check your guesses by choosing the correct idiom which corresponds to the definition you see on the left side. Be sure to use *context clues* and to use the correct grammar forms.

to die down	to get around	to break in
to come about	to fall through	to catch on
to break down	to hold on	to look on
to get ahead	to open up	to settle down
to stand out	to come up	to show up

Example:

| (to move about) | Most animals **get around** on four legs. |
| definition | correct answer |

(to happen)

1. The newspaper article didn't tell how the accident _____

_____ .

(to fail to occur)

2. The planned meeting _____ because several

members were out-of-town.

(to make progress)

3. He studied very hard in school so that he could _____

_____ in his studies.

(to be noticeable)

4. The tall building _____ against the

smaller ones.

(to stop working)

5. The workers had to work twice as hard because the large

machine had _____ .

(to diminish)

6. When the President of the U.S. entered the room, all the

noise _____ .

(to travel)

7. It is hard for people in wheelchairs to _____

because many buildings don't have elevators.

(to watch)

8. Many people _____ as firemen put out the

burning house.

(to arise)

9. In court, a question _____ about his association

with some criminals.

(to finally understand)

10. At first I was confused, but after much explanation, I

_____ .

(to wait)

11. I asked my friends, who were going out the door, to _____

_____ while I got my coat.

(to interrupt)	12. It's very impolite to _____ while someone else is speaking.
(to talk honestly)	13. Don't hide your secrets from your wife; _____ and tell her how your unhappiness came about.
(to become calm)	14. If you _____ and talk more slowly, I'll be able to understand you better; now you're too upset to think clearly.
(to arrive)	15. When the babysitter _____, my parents went out for dinner.

III. EXPLANATION OF THE IDIOMS

You probably have a good idea what each idiom means by now. Study the following explanations so that you can understand them completely.

1. **to die down**—to become more quiet; to diminish, to subside

    Usual subjects: *feelings* (excitement, nervousness, anger, love/hatred); *natural events* (storm, wind, fire); *sounds* (music, voices, noises)

    My anger at him has **died down** since he apologized to me.
    After the storm, the strong winds **died down.**
    The loud music **died down** after the police came.

2. **to come about**—to happen, to occur; to be caused

    Usual subjects: *events* (accident, death, failure/success, defeat); *situations* (problem, discussion, argument)
    This idiom is most often used in a *How-question,* when we want to know the *cause* of something.

    How did the automobile accident **come about?**
    His success **came about** after he started working harder.
    The argument **came about** because they were talking about politics.

3. **to stand out**—to be noticeable, to be prominent; to be clearly seen

    Usual subjects: color, tone; figure, shape; people

With this subject, there is a *contrast* with something else.

A very tall man wearing a big hat **stood out** in the crowd of people.
The large black letters on this small white sign really **stand out.**
Joe is so intelligent that he **stands out** in class.

4. **to break down**—to fail to function, to stop working properly

   Usual subjects: *machines* (typewriter, engine, air conditioning); *vehicles* (car, truck, plane, train, etc.)

   The travelers were delayed because the bus had **broken down.**
   It would be very regrettable if the air conditioning **broke down** on a very hot day.

5. **to fall through**—to fail to occur, not to happen

   Usual subjects: plan, project, arrangement, agreement, contract

   If your new contract agreement **falls through,** the workers in your company will go on strike.
   The plan for a new park **fell through** because no citizen wanted higher taxes.
   The project is so well planned that it couldn't possibly **fall through.**

6. **to get ahead**—to make progress, to succeed

   Usual subjects: people

   Anyone can **get ahead** in life if he or she really tries hard.
   Can a criminal **get ahead** by stealing money from a bank?
   The dream of most politicians is to **get ahead** in national politics.

7. **to get around**—to travel, to move about

   Usual subjects: *living things* (people, animals); *information* (news, idea, secret, gossip)

   It's difficult for a person with a broken leg to **get around.**
   Everyone knows him well; he really **gets around.**
   How did my secret **get around** to all my friends so quickly?

8. **to hold on**—to wait, to pause
   Usual subjects: people
   This idiom is usually used in a polite command form or in indirect speech. It is commonly used when asking someone to wait on the telephone.

Please **hold on;** I'll see if the doctor is in. (polite command)

I asked him to **hold on** before he finally left. (indirect speech)

Unusual: He **held on** before he left.

It is usually followed by a *time expression* such as "a second, a minute."

Please **hold on** a second!

Could you **hold on** a minute? (A question form is possible.)

9. **to open up**—to talk honestly and freely; to reveal a secret

Usual subjects: people

This idiom basically means that one doesn't hide his true feelings.

Their marriage plans fell through because neither one of them could ever **open up** to the other.

In court, you are expected to **open up** about what you know.

10. **to come up**—to arise

Usual subjects: a problem, question, issue

A serious problem **came up** after the project had been started.

Many questions **came up** about the quality of the project.

A political issue **came up** which embarrassed the candidate.

11. **to break in**— to interrupt (someone who is already speaking)

Usual subjects: people

While I was explaining my point of view, he **broke in** to argue with me.

During the regular TV program, the newsman **broke in** to tell about the recent disaster.

When your teacher is speaking, you shouldn't **break in.**

12. **to catch on**—to finally understand

Usual subjects: people

This idiom means that someone had difficulty in understanding something, but finally was able to understand.

After two hours of trying to learn the new game, he **caught on.**

The lady in the back of the room repeated her question several times but I still couldn't **catch on.**

13. **to look on**—to watch, to observe, to be a spectator

Usual subjects: people

I **looked on** as they tried to fix the machine which had bro-ken down.

The shopkeeper could only **look on** as the armed robbers stole all of his money.

When people are playing sports, I don't enjoy **looking on;** I would rather play also!

14. **to settle down**—1) to become calm, quiet, or peaceful
    2) to begin a normal, stable life

Usual subjects: *living things* (people, animals)

#1—The children **settled down** when their teacher entered.
The barking dogs **settled down** after the loud truck passed by.

#2—Many young people are now getting steady jobs, get-ting married, and **settling down** in their own homes.
Many people **settle down** in San Diego because of the fine weather.

15. **to show up**—to arrive, to appear

Usual subjects: people
This idiom is often used when someone appears somewhere late.

He finally **showed up** an hour late.
I hope our teacher doesn't **show up** so that we can leave.

Class discussion:

Now that you have learned the meanings of the idioms and how to use them in sentences, go back to **Exercise I** and **Exercise II** and check your answers. As you do this, consider the following questions:

1. How many idioms did you guess correctly in **Exercise I?**

2. How much better did you do in **Exercise II?**

3. Are there any idiom meanings which are still not clear to you?

4. Is there anything you have noticed about the grammatical usage of these idioms?

IV. LEARNING THE GRAMMAR RULES

Part A   Verbs are a part of English grammar which are often used in idioms. Some verbs are called *transitive* because they are followed by an object, which is always a noun phrase. Some verbs are called *intransitive* because they are not followed by an object.

Examples:

transitive verb: **to hit**

The child   hit   the ball.

subject   verb   object

intransitive verb: **to go**

Mary   goes   to her favorite restaurant   tomorrow.

subject   verb   prepositional phrase (p.p.)   time adverb

1. Can intransitive verbs be followed by other parts of grammar?

    ____ Yes   ____ No

2. What other kinds of adverbs could follow an intransitive verb?

In this chapter, verbs which are *intransitive,* because objects do not follow them, are used with words such as *around, on, through,* and *up.* Such words are called *particles* because they cannot be separated from the verbs by adverbial forms (see **Part B,** Set 2, below.) A particle joins with an intransitive verb to form an *intransitive verbal idiom.*

Example:

intransitive verb + particle: **to stand out**

A large carnation   stood out   on his suit.

subject   verbal idiom   p.p.

1. Is the verbal idiom followed by an object?

    ____ Yes   ____ No

2. Why is a word like *out* called a particle in this idiom?

Part B Look carefully at the following sets of sentences. Some sentences are correct and some are incorrect. An asterisk (*) means that a sentence is incorrect. Write your best answers to the questions by comparing the sentences.

Set 1

1. *The student got ahead his school.
2. The old man got around with difficulty.
3. *The company fell through its plan.
4. The student got ahead in school.
5. The company's plan fell through.

a. Which sentence is the correct form of #1?

b. Which sentence is the correct form of #3?

c. Circle the correct answers:

   1. The verbal idioms in this chapter (can or cannot) be followed by an object.

   2. The verbal idioms (can or cannot) be followed by a prepositional phrase.

   3. A verb which does not take an object is (transitive or intransitive).

In the incorrect sentences above (#1 and #3), the verbal idioms were followed by objects, which is not possible for intransitive forms. Other parts of grammar, such as adverbs and prepositional phrases, often occur with these verbal idioms.

Set 2

1. *My friend caught slowly on.
2. *The chairman showed early up.
3. My friend caught on slowly.
4. *The chairman early showed up.
5. My friend slowly caught on.
6. The chairman showed up early.

a. Which sentences are correct forms of #1?

b. Which sentence is the correct form of #2 and #4?

c. Try to explain why #5 is correct but #4 is incorrect: What is the difference in adverbs?

d. Circle the correct answer:

Words like *early* and *slowly* are called (adjectives or adverbs).

No adverb can be placed between the verb and particle, which shows that the verb and particle are one unit of grammar. Only a *manner* adverb, which tells how something was done (quickly, quietly, slowly), can be placed both before and after the verb + particle, if it ends in *-ly*. A manner adverb such as *well* cannot be placed before the verb + particle. Most adverbs, including time adverbs such as *early,* are placed after the idiom.

My friend caught on *slowly.*	(correct position)
My friend *slowly* caught on.	(correct position)
*My friend *well* caught on.	(incorrect position)
My friend caught on *well.*	(correct position)
*The chairman *early* showed up.	(incorrect position)
The chairman showed up *early.*	(correct position)

If you have any difficulty with the grammatical terms used in this section, such as "subject, object, noun phrase," you can refer to the **Appendix** at the end of this book for further explanation.

V. MULTIPLE-CHOICE EXERCISE

Choose the idiom which has the best meaning in the context below. No idiom is used twice as a correct answer.

1. An elephant in a circus really _____.

   a. falls through
   b. stands out
   c. shows up

2. If you weren't so careless, your typewriter wouldn't_____ _____.

   a. break down
   b. come about
   c. break in

3. He tries to _____ by studying his lessons every-

   day.

   a. die down
   b. get around
   c. get ahead

4. I'm sorry that our date with each other _____.

   a. held on
   b. got around
   c. fell through

5. If the wind _____ , we won't be able to fly our kites.

a. breaks down
b. dies down
c. opens up

6. Do you know how the murder _____ ?

a. came about
b. pitched in
c. got around

7. Because San Diego has a poor bus system, it is difficult to _____ if you don't have a car.

a. come about
b. get around
c. get ahead

8. You have to listen to me carefully if you want to _____ _____ .

a. get ahead
b. catch on
c. come up

9. Many problems _____ in our serious discussion.

a. showed up
b. came up
c. opened up

10. When Mary finally _____ we were able to leave immediately.

a. got around
b. came about
c. showed up

11. Please _____ ; you shouldn't get so upset!

a. settle down
b. die down
c. fall through

12. If you have any questions while I'm talking, feel free to _____ .

a. look on
b. come up
c. break in

13. Don't leave without me! Please _____ .

a. get ahead
b. hold on
c. catch on

VI. WRITING EXERCISE

Answer each question or statement by using the idiom in a meaningful, grammatical sentence.

1. How do you usually get around?

2. When might you wish that some noise would die down?

3. Explain why a plan might fall through.

4. To get ahead in life, what do you have to do?

5. When your car breaks down, describe what you do.

6. In your home or apartment, what stands out the most?

7. How did your desire to learn English come about?

8. When might you ask someone to hold on?

9. Why is it better to open up if you feel angry?

10. If you don't know the answer to a question which comes up in class, what do you do?

11. Why is it impolite to break in when someone is talking?

12. When a vocabulary word is very difficult, how do you try to catch on?

13. Why do some people only like to look on while others play sports?

14. What kind of life do you want when you settle down?

15. Why should people show up on time for appointments?

2

Intransitive Verbs with Prepositions

to believe in	to try for	to get over
to go into	to turn to	to go without
to run over	to go through	to part with
to run across	to turn into	to come to
to touch on	to stick to	to take after

I. GUESSING THE MEANING FROM CONTEXT

Try to guess the meaning of each idiom as it is used in the following sentences. Provide either a one-word synonym or a definition. This time, *underline the context clues* as you are trying to guess the meaning.

1. I **believe in** my wife because she always opens up to me and shows her love. _____

2. When I graduate from college, I'd like to **go into** nursing and health services as a full-time career. _____

3. Right before a test, you should **run over** your notes briefly to refresh your memory. _____

4. I was very surprised when I **ran across** Joe, an old friend I had forgotten, in the supermarket. _____

5. The TV news can only **touch on** several daily events; it can't examine them deeply. _____

6. Many athletes were **trying for** first place in the race, but only one of them could stand out as the winner. _____

7. When children need to open up about their problems, they should be able to **turn to** their parents. _____

8. The two hikers, lost in the desert, soon **went through** their entire supply of water. _____

9. Although Mike was terrible as a teenager, he has **turned into** a mature adult. _____

10. He tried to change my mind for over an hour, but I **stuck to** my own opinion. _____

11. I was quite sad about my friend's death, but slowly I **got over** it. _____

12. If you **go without** a TV in your home, you will save a lot of valuable time. _____

13. Because he moved from a house into a small apartment with no backyard, he had to **part with** his dog. _____

14. The bill for all of my grocery purchases **came to** twenty dollars. _____

15. In both physical appearance and personality, John **takes after** his father. _____

You should have discovered that the easiest way to understand the meaning of an idiom is to look at the *context* of its use. Finding the context clues first can greatly help you to limit the general meaning of the idiom, and to guess at its specific meaning. The ability to guess the meaning from context is a very important skill that you will continue to develop as you use this book.

Class discussion:

Decide which idioms were easy to guess and which were not. Discuss the importance of *context clues* in helping you to understand the meaning of each idiom.

II. DEFINITION CORRESPONDENCE

Using **Exercise I** to help you, check your guesses by choosing the correct idiom which corresponds to the definition you see on the left side. Be sure to use context clues and to use the correct grammar forms.

to believe in	to try for	to get over
to go into	to turn to	to go without
to run over	to go through	to part with
to run across	to turn into	to come to
to touch on	to stick to	to take after

(to talk briefly)   1. The President _____ many ideas in his speech;

he talked only for a short while on each idea.

(to attempt to get)   2. All the students _____ grades of "A" on the

test, but only three succeeded.

(to ask advice of)   3. If questions come up about vocabulary meaning, you can

_____ your teacher for an explanation.

(to use completely)   4. We _____ all the food in the house, so we had

to go shopping.

(to meet unexpectedly)   5. If you _____ a person who you haven't seen in

a long time, you might invite him to visit.

(to discuss carefully)   6. In the meeting, we _____ the problem area in

great detail so that everyone could catch on.

(to review)   7. The actress quickly _____ her lines in the

movie script so that she was sure of them.

(to have trust in)   8. I'm sure that the party will not fall through; I _____

_____ Ann's ability to organize it well.

(not to change)   9. If you _____ your promise to stop smoking,

you'll feel better and live longer.

(to resemble)   10. It is a biological fact that children _____ their

parents.

(to give away)   11. When he moved, he had to _____ many posses-

sions because his car was too small to carry them.

(to amount to)   12. Because I tried to get three bank loans to buy land, my

monthly payments might _____ $500.

(not to have)   13. I _____ expensive meats because I must watch

my budget if I want to get ahead.

(to recover from)   14. When I had to leave my girlfriend for six months, I felt that

I would never _____ our separation.

(to become)   15. Nice, agreeable Mary _____ a selfish, unrea-

sonable person after she won the beauty contest.

III. EXPLANATION OF THE IDIOMS

1. **to believe in**—1) to have trust or confidence in
   2) to favor, to support

   #1 Usual subjects: people
   Usual *noun phrases (NPs)*: *people* (friends, family, advisor); *qualities of people* (virtue, honesty, frankness, sincerity)

   I **believe in** Joe because he **believes in** me; in other words, we trust each other.
   Do you **believe in** your friends to help you when you need it?

   #2 Usual subjects: people
   Usual NPs: idea, situation, plan
   For definition #2, the NP is often a *verb + ing* form.

   The President **believes in** the idea of a world government.
   If you **believe in** joining our political party, you should donate some money.

2. **to go into**—to examine, to consider, to discuss (in detail)

   Usual subjects: people; lecture, speech, book, discussion
   Usual NPs: problem, question; issue, topic; details

   In his speech, the president **went into** the many problems of the company.
   The President's speech **went into** the many problems of the economy.
   This book **goes into** the life of Albert Einstein in much detail.
   The topic was so interesting that our discussion **went into** its many aspects for several hours.

3. **to run over**—to review; to rehearse

   Usual subjects: people
   Usual NPs: notes, minutes (of a meeting); part (in a play)

The teacher **ran over** his notes before he gave his lecture.
Run over your part in the play at least three times before we rehearse it together.
You should **run over** new vocabulary every night.

4. **to run across**—to meet (someone) or to find (something) unexpectedly

Usual subjects: people
Usual NPs: *people* (old friend, forgotten classmate); things

While he was looking on at the football game he **ran across** an old classmate from his high school days.
I **ran across** some old pictures in the garage which I hadn't seen in years.
In the library, I **ran across** a good reference for my term paper.

5. **to touch on**—to talk briefly about; to discuss superficially

Usual subjects: *people* (author, speaker, teacher); book lecture
Usual NPs: subject, topic, question, idea

In his book, the author only **touched on** the reasons for his ideas; he didn't go into them deeply.
The professor's lecture **touched on** the most important ideas we had to know for the test; it was mainly a review lecture.
Even though I wanted to know all the details about my illness, the doctor only **touched on** them and then quickly discussed medicine.

6. **to try for**—to attempt to win; to try to get

Usual subjects: people
Usual NPs: *award* (prize, medal); record; *position* (job, post, employment)

In a contest, everyone usually **tries for** first place.
He **tried for** a new record by running faster than anyone else in the world.
I've **tried for** several jobs, but they have all fallen through.
Inexperienced workers who **try for** employment which requires special skills usually fail.

7. **to turn to**—to ask help of; to get advice from

Usual subjects: people
Usual NPs: *people* (friend, parent, classmate, teacher); notes, encyclopedia, dictionary

You should **turn to** your wife and open up if you are having marital problems.

Too many students **turn to** the dictionary to learn the meaning of a word instead of trying to catch on from the context.

8. **to go through**—to use completely; to spend, to waste

Usual subjects: people
Usual NPs: food, supplies; money, fortune

In two days we **went through** all the food we had bought for our four-day camping trip.
The store **went through** its whole supply of the popular sale item.
The spoiled grandson soon **went through** the fortune he had inherited.

9. **to turn into**—to change into, to become

Usual subjects: *living things* (people, animals); a changeable item
Usual NPs: same as above
This idiom is used when the subject experiences a major change in appearance or structure. For people or animals, this could include personality.

The young boy **turned into** a mature adult.
Joe used to be a very agreeable, friendly person, but now he has **turned into** a disagreeable, stubborn person.
Water can **turn into** steam or ice.

10. **to stick to**—to never change or abandon; to hold to, to keep

Usual subjects: people
Usual NPs: *mental concept* (idea, principle, belief); decision, choice

Your friends don't know everything; **stick to** your own ideas when you think that you are right.
Church organizations expect people to **stick to** their religious principles.
They tried to change my mind repeatedly, but I **stuck to** my first choice.

11. **to get over**—to recover from, to become normal after

Usual subjects: living things
Usual NPs: *ailment* (cold, disease, illness, sickness); *feeling* (surprise, shock; disappointment; love/hatred)

When do you think that you'll **get over** your illness?
Will he ever **get over** his love for the woman who left him?

It was hard for me to **get over** the disappointment of losing the job I had tried for.

12. **to go without**—not to have, to lack; to do without

Usual subjects: living things
Usual NPs: *necessities of life* (food, clothes, water, housing)

Many poor people in the world have to **go without** life's necessities.
Lost in the desert, the men had **gone without** food or water for five days.
People who go through their money quickly often have to **go without** essentials.

13. **to part with**—to give away; to sell; to separate (oneself) from

Usual subjects: people
Usual NPs: *personal possessions* (money, car, animals, furniture, etc.)

I had to **part with** my car because the monthly payments were too high.
My cat was eating all my houseplants so I had to **part with** it.
I would hate to **part with** my antiques if I moved to a smaller place.

14. **to come to**—to amount to, to be equal to, to total (a numerical figure)

Usual subjects: total, bill, account; purchases; rent
Usual NPs: some quantity or monetary figure

Because of inflation, my weekly food bill now **comes to** $30.
All of my purchases in the store **came to** $50.
The number of students in this class **comes to** fifteen.

15. **to take after**—to resemble, to look like

Usual subjects: people
Usual NPs: *family* (father, mother, grandparents)

In personality, he **takes after** his mother, not his father.
Tom **takes after** his father. They both have red hair and freckles.

Class discussion:

Now that you have learned the meanings of the idioms and how to use them in sentences, go back to **Exercise I** and **Exercise II** and check your answers. As you do this, consider the following questions:

1. How many idioms did you guess correctly in **Exercise I?**

2. How much better did you do in **Exercise II?**

3. Are there any idiom meanings which are still not clear to you?

4. Is there anything you have noticed about the grammatical usage of these idioms?

IV. LEARNING THE GRAMMAR RULES

Part A   All of the idioms in this chapter are composed of an *intransitive verb + preposition*. The preposition is followed by a noun phrase, and together they form a prepositional phrase.

Example:

intransitive verb + preposition: **to touch on**

prepositional phrase

The lecturer touched on many interesting ideas.

subject   verbal idiom

1. Circle the correct answers:

   a. The preposition *on* is connected to the noun phrase in (meaning or grammar).

   b. The preposition *on* is connected to the intransitive verb in (meaning or grammar).

2. Is the verbal idiom followed by an object?

   _____ Yes   _____ No

How did you decide?

The preceding questions require some explanation. The prepositional phrase, "on many interesting ideas" is a unit of *grammar;* the verbal idiom **touch on** is a unit of special *meaning*. An intransitive verbal idiom is never used with an object.

Part B Look carefully at the following set of sentences. Some sentences are correct and some are incorrect. An asterisk (*) means that a sentence is incorrect. As you did before, answer the questions by comparing the sentences.

1. The teacher touched quickly on many ideas.
2. *Because she is my friend, I believe in.
3. The teacher quickly touched on many ideas.
4. Because she is my friend, I believe in her.
5. *The teacher touched on quickly many ideas.
6. The guests finally showed up.

a. Which sentences are correct forms of #5?

b. Which sentence is the correct form of #2?

c. In #2, what part of grammar is needed to make the sentence correct?

d. Circle the correct answers:

    a. In sentence #4, *in* is a (particle or preposition).

    b. In sentence #6, *up* is a (particle or preposition).

Adverbs may not be placed between a preposition and noun phrase, which shows that the preposition and noun phrase are a grammatical unit. Adverbs may be placed between the intransitive verb and preposition, but *not* between an intransitive verb + particle such as **to show up.** (see **Chapter 1**)

The teacher *quickly* touched on many ideas. (correct position)
The teacher touched *quickly* on many ideas. (correct position)
*The teacher touched on *quickly* many ideas. (incorrect position)
The guests *finally* showed up   (correct position)
*The guests showed *finally* up.   (incorrect position)

Sometimes, the same word can serve as a preposition or as a particle, depending on the grammar and meaning of the verbal idiom.

Compare:

The teacher touched *on* many ideas.

    (Here *on* is a *preposition* which forms a unit of meaning with the intransitive verb, but a unit of grammar with the following noun phrase.)

The student finally caught *on.*

(Here *on* is a *particle* which is connected to the intransitive verb in both meaning and grammar.)

There is no easy way to know when a word is a particle and when it is a preposition. Through practice, you will have to learn and remember the various rules for the grammar of verbal idioms.

V. MULTIPLE-CHOICE EXERCISE

Choose the idiom from **Chapters 1** and **2** which has the best meaning in each context below. No idiom is used twice as a correct answer. Be very careful about the grammar rules which you have learned.

1. I prefer to _____ one topic in great detail, instead of touching on many topics.
   a. run over
   b. go into
   c. catch on

2. What a surprise it was to _____ Joe after so many years!
   a. run across
   b. show up
   c. run over

3. He thinks that this idea is true; I _____ the other idea.
   a. catch on
   b. touch on
   c. believe in

4. Save your money! Don't _____ it too quickly.
   a. die down
   b. hold on
   c. go through

5. Your purple pants and pink shirt really _____.
   a. stand out
   b. run over
   c. try for

6. I sat nearby and _____ as he played the piano for me.
   a. came up
   b. turned into
   c. looked on

7. He's so stubborn that he _____ all his opinions.
   a. goes without
   b. sticks to
   c. takes after

8. If a difficult question comes up, a teacher should do more than _____ it briefly.
   a. go into
   b. touch on
   c. open up

9. Don't _____ impolitely! I was talking first.

    a. get around
    b. look into
    c. break in

10. He went back to work after he had _____ his cold.

    a. gotten over
    b. fallen through
    c. died down

11. He had an appointment with me but he never _____ .

    a. turned into
    b. showed up
    c. came to

12. Small streams can _____ rivers when winter snow melts.

    a. part with
    b. go without
    c. turn into

13. It's hard to _____ in a car when the streets are very crowded.

    a. get ahead
    b. go through
    c. get around

VI. WRITING EXERCISE

Answer each question or statement by using the idiom in a meaningful, grammatical sentence.

1. What religion do you believe in?

2. How often do you run over your classwork at home?

3. When was the last time that you ran across an old friend?

4. Do you prefer to touch on your personal problems or do you prefer to really go into them when you are talking with your friends? Why?

5. When was the last time you tried for something but you failed?

6. Whom do you turn to when you have a problem?

7. Do you go through money quickly or slowly? Why?

8. If you could turn into an animal, which animal would it be?

9. Do you stick to your plans or do you often let them fall through?

10. What was the last illness or emotional problem which you got over?

11. If you were poor, what would you have to go without?

12. Suddenly you need some money and you have to sell something; what will you part with?

13. What does your monthly food bill come to?

14. Which parent do you take after? In what way?

3

Intransitive Verbs with Particles and Prepositions

to put up with	to look up to	to be in on
to look forward to	to cut down on	to look out for
to come up with	to live up to	to keep up with
to go in for	to do away with	to look back on
to get through to	to run around with	to work up to

I. GUESSING THE MEANING FROM CONTEXT

Try to guess the meaning of each idiom as it is used in the following sentences. Provide either a one-word synonym or a definition. Underline the context clues as you are trying to guess the meaning.

1. I can **put up with** some noise while I'm studying, but I can't accept loud noise. _____

2. I have been working so hard that I'm **looking forward to** a nice, relaxing vacation. _____

3. We tried for hours to solve our problem; Sally **came up with** an answer after she studied the problem carefully. _____

4. Some people **go in for** sports like football, while other people **go in for** hobbies like reading. _____

5. The idea was too difficult and he couldn't catch on to my explanation; I could never **get through to** him. _____

6. You can **look up to** a teacher who really wants to help you and always does his or her best. _____

7. To lose weight, you have to **cut down on** sugar and other sweet things. _____

8. Because he did a very poor job and came up with bad results, his boss felt that he hadn't **lived up to** his responsibilities. _____

9. It's not enough to cut down on atomic bomb production; we must **do away with** it completely. _____

10. During all four years of high school, I **ran around with** the same group of friends; we did everything together. _____

11. Her social schedule was very busy, and she liked to **be in on** every party or activity. _____

12. When driving near a school, **look out for** children crossing the road. _____

13. My body was well-prepared for the ten-mile race, so I was able to **keep up with** the other runners. _____

14. My grandmother tells me many interesting historical facts when she **looks back on** her youth. _____

15. Tom began as a local salesman, but after thirty years with the same company he had **worked up to** sales manager. _____

Class discussion:

Decide which idioms were easy to guess and which were not. Discuss the importance of context clues in helping you to understand the meaning of each idiom.

II. DEFINITION CORRESPONDENCE

Using **Exercise I** to help you, check your guesses by choosing the correct idiom which corresponds to the definition you see on the left side. Be sure to use context clues and to use the correct grammar forms.

to put up with	to look up to	to be in on
to look forward to	to cut down on	to look out for
to come up with	to live up to	to keep up with
to go in for	to do away with	to look back on
to get through to	to run around with	to work up to

(to make one understand) 1. My explanation of the idea was so clear that I _____

_____ him immediately.

(to reduce the use of) 2. After his heart attack, he had to _____ smoking and drinking.

(to admire greatly) 3. Americans usually _____ a President who is sincere and does the best possible job.

(to anticipate)

4. Cindy has worked so hard this week that she _____ _____ an exciting Friday evening.

(to be interested in)

5. It is very popular now to _____ running; thousands of people are doing it.

(to tolerate)

6. The people of California couldn't _____ high taxes, so they voted to lower property taxes.

(to find)

7. For a long time I couldn't _____ a good subject for my term paper, but finally I was able to think of one.

(to maintain the same rate as)

8. Some men think that women workers can't _____ _____ male workers, but I know many women who work equally as well.

(to participate in)

9. I'd like to _____ all your planning and decisions; I have some ideas I'd like to share with you.

(to watch for)

10. On a crowded train, you should _____ people who might try to steal your luggage or wallet.

(to associate with)

11. Mrs. Smith's son was out of the house very often, so she didn't know that he was _____ a group of wild teenagers.

(to fulfill a responsibility)

12. He promised to pay back his $20 debt to me, and I am glad to say that now he has _____ his promise.

(to abolish)

13. It's very sad that some people are still so poor in the world; when can we _____ poverty so that everyone lives comfortably?

(to remember the past)

14. When my brother was in Europe, he had many fine experi-

ences; now he _____ that trip with great plea-

sure as he tells other people about it.

(to advance to)   15. Jane is going back to school so that she can learn more and

_____ a position in higher management.

III. EXPLANATION OF THE IDIOMS

1. **to put up with**—to tolerate, to accept unwillingly

   Usual subjects: people
   Usual NPs: *annoyance* (noise, disturbance, music); *bad behavior* (manners, attitude, impoliteness); people
   This idiom means that the person does not like something but has to accept it, for some reason.

   When you're trying to sleep, it's hard to **put up with** noise.
   I can't **put up with** the children's shouting and pushing.
   Can you **put up with** Jerry when he's in a bad mood? I can't.

2. **to look forward to**—to anticipate with pleasure

   Usual subjects: people
   Usual NPs: *situation* (going somewhere, doing something); *a special occasion* (holiday, vacation, birthday, party, date)
   This idiom means that the person likes something in the future, and thinks about it with pleasure. This idiom is often followed by a *verb + ing* form.

   I **look forward to** getting many gifts next Christmas.
   Do you **look forward to** your next vacation or are you too busy working to think about it?
   I've been trying to meet that woman for a long time, so I'm really **looking forward to** our first date.

3. **to come up with**—to suggest, to offer; to find

   Usual subjects: people
   Usual NPs: *mental concepts* (idea, plan, information; answer, solution, suggestion)

   No one in class could find an answer, but finally Joe **came up with** one.
   The scientist **came up with** a good plan for using solar energy.
   In a foreign language classroom, you should try to **come up with** good answers as often as possible, if you want to get ahead.

4. **to go in for**—to be interested in; to play (as a sport)

Usual subjects: people
Usual NPs: *hobby* (reading, chess, etc.); *sports* (football, soccer, etc.)
This idiom is often followed by a *verb + ing* form.

She **goes in for** reading intelligent, interesting books.
Some people **go in for** sports for good exercise.
If you **go in for** cooking, you'll probably gain weight.

5. **to get through to**—to make (someone) understand; to communicate successfully

Usual subjects: people
Usual NPs: people
This idiom means that the person (subject) cannot explain something so that someone (the NP) can understand, but finally succeeds.

I spent hours trying to **get through to** him; I was surprised that he never caught on.
He never wants to talk about his problem; I've tried to **get through to him,** but he won't open up.
My affection never pleased her, so I couldn't **get through to** her.

6. **to look up to**—to respect, to admire greatly

Usual subjects: people
Usual NPs: *people* (boss, parents, big brother, friend)

A manager should always try to make his workers **look up to** him.
If a child does not **look up to** his parents, they probably are not very good to him.
Look up to your friends who are eager to help you.
Younger children often **look up to** their older brothers or sisters for advice.

7. **to cut down on**—to reduce the use of, to lessen

Usual subjects: people; company, business, government
Usual NPs: eating, drinking, smoking; spending, wasting, use
This idiom is often followed by a *verb + ing* form.

Overweight people should **cut down on** eating.
Shouldn't the government **cut down on** wasteful spending?
The small business **cut down on** its use of electricity in order to save money.

8. **to live up to**—to complete a responsibility, to equal an expected standard

Usual subjects: people
Usual NPs: responsibility, duty (of people); promise, claim, standard (for people or machines)

When you get a job, your new boss expects you to **live up to** your responsibilities.
She had agreed to work while her husband finished school, and she **lived up to** her promise by supporting both of them.
This machine works very well; it **lives up to** the company's claim.

9. **to do away with**—to abolish, to get rid of

Usual subjects: people; government, state
Usual NPs: rule, tax, law; a bad situation which has existed for a long time (slavery, war, discrimination, dictatorship, crime)

The state legislature **did away with** the death penalty; now the state can't punish criminals severely.
Governments could not survive if the people voted to **do away with** all taxes.
The police are trying to **do away with** crime, but the underworld is very strong.

10. **to run around with**—to associate with regularly, to hang around with

Usual subjects: people
Usual NPs: people

After work, do you **run around with** the people from your company?
If you **run around with** bad people, you'll turn into a criminal too.
High school students **run around with** their classmates after school.

11. **to be in on**—to participate in, to have a share in; to know (a secret)

Usual subjects: people
Usual NPs: activity, plan, venture; idea, suggestion, secret

We need one more person for our trip, so let's ask Joe to **be in on** it.
The meeting is very important, so the company president will **be in on** it.

If you **are in on** a friend's secret, you shouldn't open up to others.

12. **to look out for**—to watch for; to be careful of

Usual subjects: living things
Usual NPs: an important thing or idea; danger, warning; people

While you are reading, **look out for** unfamiliar vocabulary to learn.
When driving, you should **look out for** dangerous road conditions.
Policemen, who try to stop crime, have to **look out for** criminals.

13. **to keep up with**—maintain the same rate as, to do with the same amount of energy

Usual subjects: people; salary, wages
Usual NPs: people; prices, cost of living, inflation

My legs are so short that I have trouble **keeping up with** other runners.
If you do your homework everyday, you can **keep up with** your classmates.
Because of inflation, salaries can't **keep up with** the high cost of living.

14. **to look back on**—to remember something from one's past, to reminisce

Usual subjects: people
Usual NPs: youth, childhood; event, time, change

When I **look back on** my college years, I'm surprised that I graduated!
Looking back on my childhood, I can still come up with many interesting events that happened to me.

15. **to work up to**—to advance to, to rise to

Usual subjects: people
Usual NPs: a higher position or level

John **worked up to** supervisor after twenty years as assistant.
I think that you can **work up to** a higher score on the next test.

Class discussion:

Now that you have learned the meanings of the idioms and how to use them in sentences, go back to **Exercise I** and **Exercise II** and check your answers. As you do this, consider the following questions:

1. How many idioms did you guess correctly in **Exercise I?**

2. How much better did you do in **Exercise II?**

3. Are there any idiom meanings which are still not clear to you?

4. Is there anything you have noticed about the grammatical usage of these idioms?

IV. LEARNING THE GRAMMAR RULES

Part A   All of the idioms in this chapter are composed of an *intransitive verb + particle + preposition*. The preposition is followed by a noun phrase, forming a prepositional phrase.

Example:

intransitive verb + particle + preposition: **to come up with**

John came up with a fine solution.

1. Is the verbal idiom followed by an object?

    _____ Yes   _____ No

2. What follows the preposition; and are they joined in meaning or in grammar?

3. Is the preposition joined to the verb and particle in meaning or in grammar?

If you had any problem with these questions, you should review the grammar sections of **Chapters 1** and **2.**

Part B   Look carefully at the following set of sentences. Some are correct and some are incorrect (*). Answer the questions by comparing the sentences.

1. A student's question came up.
2. *A student came up a question.
3. A student came up with a question.
4. I greatly look forward to my vacation.
5. *I look greatly forward to my vacation.
6. I look forward greatly to my vacation.
7. *I look forward to greatly my vacation.

a. Which sentences are the correct forms of sentence #2?

b. What is the difference between the idioms in sentence #1 and sentence #3?

c. Which sentences are correct forms of sentences #5 and #7?

d. Circle the correct answers:

In the idiom **come up with,** *up* is a (particle or preposition) and *with* is a (particle or preposition).

e. Fill in the appropriate answers:

   1. An adverb can be placed between a _____

   and _____ _____ , or before a _____ if

   the adverb ends in *-ly.*

   2. An adverb should *not* be placed between a _____

   and _____ , or between a _____

   and _____ .

These rules show us that the verb, particle, and preposition are all connected in *meaning* but that, in *grammar,* the particle is connected to the verb and the preposition to the noun phrase. That is why an adverb, especially a manner adverb, can sometimes be placed between the particle and preposition.

I *greatly* look forward to my vacation.   (correct position)
I look forward *greatly* to my vacation.   (correct position)
*I look forward to *greatly* my vacation.   (incorrect position)
*I look *greatly* forward to my vacation.   (incorrect position)

V. MULTIPLE-CHOICE EXERCISE

Choose the idiom from this chapter, or a previous one, which has the best meaning in the context below. No idiom is used twice as a correct answer. Be very careful about the grammar rules which you have learned.

1. Joe tries hard, but he doesn't catch on easily; sometimes it's difficult to _____ him.

   a. look forward to
   b. get through to
   c. try for

2. You really cough too much; you should _____ smoking.

   a. take after
   b. go in for
   c. cut down on

3. The careless typist _____ too much paper because she made so many mistakes.

   a. went through
   b. went without
   c. parted with

4. I didn't know you were in town! It's strange to _____ you like this.

   a. look forward to
   b. run across
   c. put up with

5. All the yelling and screaming _____ when the police entered with their guns out.

   a. showed up
   b. broke in
   c. died down

6. Don't worry about tomorrow's test; _____ and relax!

   a. settle down
   b. die down
   c. get over

7. I'll go back to work, when I _____ this sickness.

   a. turn into
   b. get over
   c. go without

8. The two doctor bills _____ an amazing $5,000.

   a. came to
   b. touched on
   c. opened up

9. The citizens had wanted more freedom so they _____ the dictatorial government in the last election.

   a. were in on
   b. did away with
   c. looked up to

10. If you stick to your promise, you'll undoubtedly _____ it.

    a. live up to
    b. fall through
    c. come to

11. He only _____ the problem; he didn't go into it carefully.

    a. got over
    b. touched on
    c. settled down

12. The thief had to _____ the police because they were all around him.

a. work up to
b. run across
c. look out for

13. They work hard, and too quickly for me to _____ _____ them.

a. get over
b. keep up with
c. work up to

VI. WRITING EXERCISE

Answer each question or statement by using the idiom in a meaningful, grammatical sentence.

1. As a student, you have to put up with many problems. Name one.

2. What special event are you looking forward to in the near future?

3. In class, why should you come up with good answers?

4. Do you go in for hobbies or for sports?

5. Why is it difficult to get through to some people?

6. In your family, who do you look up to?

7. Why do some people cut down on exercise instead of increasing it?

8. Are you trying to live up to any promise you've made to yourself? What was that promise?

9. What problem in your native country would you do away with, if you were the country's leader?

10. Do you run around with friends from your country or from the United States? Why?

11. Are you in on any of your friends' secrets?

12. When you're driving, what do you have to look out for?

13. Why is it easy or difficult for you to keep up with your class-mates?

14. Which part of your life do you look back on most often?

15. Why would a politician want to work up to the Presidency of the U.S.?

4

Review of Intransitive Verbal Idioms

I. COMPARISON OF INTRANSITIVE FORMS

Verbal idioms are very useful, and very commonly used in English, because various verbs can join with different particles and/or prepositions to form unique combinations of meaning. In this first section there are several intransitive verbal idioms which can change form and meaning.

A One very common change occurs when a *preposition* is added to certain *intransitive verb + particle* combinations. You were shown an example of this in the grammar exercise of **Chapter 3** (page 34). The idiom **come up,** meaning "to arise, to be asked," can join with the preposition *with* to form **come up with,** meaning "to suggest, to offer."

His suggestion **came up** in class.
He **came up with** a suggestion in class.

Only some verb + particle idioms can join with a preposition in this way, so you have to learn the idioms which can. Three other idioms from **Chapter 1** can join with prepositions in this way, and the preposition is followed by a noun phrase.

1. **to catch on**—to finally understand
   to catch on to—(same meaning)

   The lecture was difficult, but eventually Jim **caught on.**
   Jim eventually **caught on to** the difficult lecture.

2. **to break in**—to interrupt
   to break in on—(same meaning)

   We were having a conversation but he **broke in.**
   He **broke in on** our conversation.

3. **to stand out**—to be noticeable
   to stand out from—(same meaning)

   In the large crowd a tall man **stood out.**
   A tall man **stood out from** the large crowd.

In the case of these forms, it happens that there is no change of meaning, but this is not always so. You have to be careful to note when a change in meaning occurs so that you don't use the idiom incorrectly.

The difference between **come up** and **come up with** is one good example of this.

B You probably can guess that many of the *verb + particle + preposition* idioms in **Chapter 3** were made by adding a preposition to an intransitive verb + particle form. The idiom **come up with** was one example. There are six other verbal idioms you have studied which are used both with and without a preposition. When a preposition *is* used, a *noun phrase* will follow.

1. **to look back on**—to remember (one's past)
   to look back—(same meaning)

   When I **look back on** that trip, I remember nice things.
   Looking back, I remember many nice things about that trip.

2. **to keep up with**—to maintain the same rate as
   to keep up—to maintain the same rate

   I couldn't **keep up with** Joe because he was running too quickly.
   Because Joe was running too quickly, I couldn't **keep up.**

3. **to look out for**—to be careful of
   to look out—to be careful

   I told him to **look out for** rattlesnakes in the rocks.
   Look out! There's a rattlesnake in those rocks.

4. **to be in on**—to participate in
   to be in—to be popular, fashionable

   Everyone would like to **be in on** the first passenger flight to the moon.
   Long skirts **are in** during some years and short skirts **are in** during other years.

5. **to look up to**—to respect
   to look up—to improve

   Everyone **looks up to** him because he is always so helpful.
   My life is more enjoyable because my financial situation is **looking up.**

In the case of the fourth and fifth idioms above, there is a very big difference in meaning between the form with a preposition and the form without a preposition. It is easy to see that these forms are truly idiomatic because such a small word as *on* or *to* causes such a very big difference in meaning.

There is no quick way of learning when a preposition changes the meaning and when it doesn't; you must be careful to pay attention to such variations and do your best to learn each special situation.

II. OTHER GRAMMATICAL FORMS OF INTRANSITIVE VERBAL IDIOMS

To be able to use verbal idioms in many different situations, you should know how to transform the idioms into other grammatical forms. In this chapter we will look at two of the most important forms.

A. Nominalized Forms

Sometimes it is useful to change a verbal idiom into a nominalized form. In this case, an *intransitive verb + particle* or an *intransitive verb + preposition* can combine to form a noun.

Only one of the intransitive idioms in this book is commonly used in a noun form. Compare the following:

I was late because the bus **broke down.**
I was late because of a bus **breakdown.**

However, this form is common with other intransitive idioms which you have not studied. Compare the following:

Did the plane **take off** smoothly?
Did the plane have a smooth **take-off?**

The baseball players **warmed up** before the game.
The baseball players had a **warm-up** before the game.

We **stopped over** at the nice motel on our trip.
We made a **stopover** at the nice motel on our trip.

Notice that some forms use a hyphen (-) and other forms don't. Be sure to remember that only some intransitive verbal idioms can use this transformation. You have to learn and memorize the special rules as you study new verbal idioms if you want to be able to use them correctly.

B. Passive Forms

Sometimes the subject of a verbal idiom is not very important, and we want to stress the noun phrase which follows the particle or preposition. Noun phrases following *intransitive verb + preposition* forms or *intransitive verb + particle + preposition* forms may be moved to subject position after the unimportant subject has either been moved to the end of the sentence or removed completely. The verbal idiom would be changed from the active to the passive form, just as a regular verb would.

Compare the following examples:

The police **looked into** the murder.
The murder **was looked into** by the police.
The murder **was looked into.**

We finally **dealt with** our problem.
Our problem **was** finally **dealt with** (by us).

The students had to **put up with** the noise.
The noise had to **be put up with** (by the students).

Many people **looked up to** the famous professor.
The famous professor was **looked up to** (by many people).

Not all idioms can be put into a passive form, simply because some idioms sound strange or awkward in such form. Notice the unacceptability of the following sentences:

We **went in for** soccer.
*Soccer **was gone in for** (by us).

Mary **takes after** her mom.
*Mary's mom **is taken after** (by Mary).

There is really no simple explanation as to why some verbal idioms can easily be made passive and others can't. You simply have to acquire this knowledge by paying attention to and carefully learning the uses of this passive construction as you learn new and different idioms.

III. PARAGRAPH COMPOSITION

Please write a short paragraph using each group of idioms listed below. Organize your thoughts before you start to write so that the paragraph is logical and well-organized. A situation is suggested for your use.

A. A group of people had a discussion about a difficult theory.

(to go into, to get through to, to break in, to come up with)

_____

_____

_____

_____

_____

_____

_____

B. A motorist was standing by his car on the side of the road.

(to break down, to look out for, to show up, to turn to)

_____

_____

_____

_____

_____

_____

_____

C. Someone is talking about his life history and his memories.

(to look back on, to settle down, to get ahead, to work up to)

_____

_____

_____

_____

_____

_____

_____

D. Someone is talking about his financial difficulties, which were caused by losing a job.

(to fall through, to go without, to go through, to part with)

_____

_____

_____

_____

_____

_____

_____

IV. ADDITIONAL CLASS ACTIVITIES

A. Role-Play Topics

One of the best ways to gain experience in using idioms in conversation is to create a real-life situation where they might be found. The class should divide into small groups, and each group should create a dialogue which incorporates the suggested topic(s) and appropriate idioms. If possible, the groups should take turns presenting their dialogues to the rest of the class. Differences in the presentations should be discussed.

1. You are a motorist whose car broke down on the side of the road and you are now back at home talking with your friends about your serious engine problem. What is your conversation?

    Suggested idioms: get around, cut down on, go without, part with

2. A couple of students are having a study session. They are talking about the difficulty of their schoolwork and their efforts to succeed in school. What do they say?

    Suggested idioms: get ahead, catch on, keep up with, stick to

3. John and Mary are a married couple who are having some small problems in their marriage. They are discussing the ways they can improve their relationship. What do they say to each other?

   Suggested idioms: come about, open up, put up with, live up to

B. Discussion Topics

1. How did you feel while you were presenting your dialogue to the rest of the class? Did your "acting" feel natural or unnatural? Did you feel comfortable using the idioms in your presentation?

2. Why do you think that idiomatic expressions are so common in every language? In your opinion, is this good or bad?

3. What are some very common idiomatic expressions in your own language? Explain them, in English, to your classmates.

4. Do some of the idioms you have learned in this book have a similar form in your own language? Which ones? What are the similarities or differences?

5. When you have opportunities to talk with English speakers, or to listen to, or read material in English (such as books, movies, television, etc.), try to note the use of idioms and bring in a few examples to class for discussion.

II

TRANSITIVE
VERBAL IDIOMS

5
Transitive Verbs with Movable Particles

to make up   to clear up   to look up
to think over   to put off   to point out
to bring up   to carry out   to talk over
to give away   to bring about   to make out
to try out   to call off   to take off

I. GUESSING THE MEANING FROM CONTEXT

Guess the meaning of each idiom as it is used in the following sentences. Provide either a one-word synonym or a definition. Underline the context clues as you are trying to guess the meaning.

1. Nothing he told me was true; I'm angry that he **made up** the whole story.   _____

2. I'll **think over** your idea carefully before I make a final decision about it.   _____

3. If you **bring up** a question in class, I'm sure that your teacher can come up with an answer for you.   _____

4. Sometimes a business will **give away** free samples of their product so that people can learn about it.   _____

5. Be sure to **try out** a new car before you buy it; look out for problems in advance.   _____

6. Many students couldn't catch on, but the teacher **cleared up** the problem by going into a detailed explanation.   _____

7. He **put off** his work until later, instead of doing it right away.   _____

8. You have always **carried out** your duties well so I am going to give you a raise.   _____

9. How did the accident happen? That man **brought about** the accident when he hit the other car.

_____

10. The tour organization **called off** the trip because so few people showed up at the first orientation meeting.

_____

11. I went to the library to **look up** some information to use in my term paper.

_____

12. He tried to get through to me by **pointing out** the mistakes in my paper.

_____

13. When people open up to each other, they usually **talk over** their problems.

_____

14. It was too dark to **make out** the letters on the sign far ahead.

_____

15. I've been working too hard lately; it's time for me to **take off** a couple of weeks of vacation.

_____

Class discussion:

Decide which idioms were easy to guess and which were not. Discuss the importance of context clues in helping you to understand the meaning of each idiom.

II. DEFINITION CORRESPONDENCE

Using **Exercise I** to help you, check your guesses by choosing the correct idiom which corresponds to the definition you see on the left side. Be sure to use context clues and to use the correct grammar forms.

to make up	to clear up	to look up
to think over	to put off	to point out
to bring up	to carry out	to talk over
to give away	to bring about	to make out
to try out	to call off	to take off

(to consider carefully)   1. You should _____ an important matter before

you finally decide on it.

(to distribute freely)   2. The new restaurant _____ prizes to its first 100

customers as an advertising method.

(to accomplish)   3. The spy successfully _____ his assignment in

the enemy country, returning safely to his country after it

was completed.

(to test)   4. Jeff _____ each machine and the best one soon

stood out, so he bought it.

(to postpone)   5. Because a rainstorm was expected, we _____

our baseball game for two days.

(to cause)   6. The child _____ the fire in the house because

he played with matches.

(to introduce)   7. We thought our plan was perfect, but at the last moment

someone _____ a serious problem.

(to invent)   8. If you _____ an excuse for being late to class,

the teacher might not believe in your honesty.

(to make clear)   9. At first I couldn't get through to the student, but finally I

_____ his confusion.

(to discuss)   10. Mary had to _____ her travel problems with

the airline manager.

(to cancel)   11. The president _____ the special meeting be-

cause there was no longer any need for it.

(to have free time off) 12. The employee _____ the summer to travel with

his family.

(to distinguish)   13. With my new glasses I can _____ every-

thing much better than before.

(to try to find)   14. He turned to a bigger dictionary to _____ the

exact definition of the word.

(to indicate)   15. Mr. James _____ many examples of the dif-

ficult theory, and soon the confused students caught on.

III. EXPLANATION OF THE IDIOMS

1. **to make up**—1) to invent, to fabricate (a lie)
                          2) to apply cosmetics

   #1 Usual subjects: people
      Usual objects: lie, excuse, story, the whole thing

      It's a bad habit to **make up** lies about things which you
         know are wrong; no one will believe you.
      He told me a strange story about his illness, and I think
         that he **made** the whole thing **up.**

   #2 Usual subjects: *people* (actor, clown, woman)
      Usual objects: face, nose

      Many women like to **make up** their face each morning.
      The clown **makes up** his nose with red paint.

2. **to think over**—to consider carefully, to ponder

   Usual subjects: people
   Usual objects: plan, suggestion, offer; problem, matter
   This idiom is used when the subject doesn't want to make a
      quick, careless decision.

   I wanted to **think over** their plan before I agreed to follow
      it.
   Think over your problems before you finally decide what to
      do.

3. **to bring up**—1) to introduce, to present, to raise
                          2) to rear, to raise

   #1 Usual subjects: people
      Usual objects: question, problem; matter, subject, point
      This idiom is very close in meaning to **to come up with.**

      When you want to go into a subject more carefully in
         class, you should **bring up** many questions.
      When the president **brought up** the energy matter, the
         committee looked into it carefully.

   #2 Usual subjects: *people* (parents, nurse, grandmother,
         foster home)
      Usual objects: child, daughter, son

      Parents should **bring up** their children with love and
         devotion.
      Grandmother Johnson **brought up** her little grand-
         daughter when her son and daughter-in-law were lost
         at sea.

4. **to give away**—1) to distribute freely, to give at no cost
2) to reveal, to tell (a secret)

#1 Usual subjects: people; company, business
Usual objects: prize, gift, sample product; personal possession

The popular game shows **give away** many prizes and gifts to the contestants on TV.
In supermarkets, food companies often **give away** samples of their products to customers.

#2 Usual subjects: people
Usual objects: secret, hidden fact

He **gave** my age **away** even though I had told him not to tell anyone.
This fact is my own private matter; you shouldn't have **given away** my secret.

5. **to try out**—to test, to check the function of

Usual subjects: people
Usual objects: *machine* (car, typewriter, television, etc.)

You should always **try out** a car before you buy it so that you can look out for serious problems.
After the secretary **tried out** the typewriter for fifteen minutes she could see that it would soon break down.

6. **to clear up**—to make clear, to clarify, to remove doubt about

Usual subjects: people; explanation
Usual objects: difficulty, misunderstanding, confusion, problem; matter, point

When a student cannot catch on to an idea, the teacher should try to **clear up** his misunderstanding.
Jane and I argued for a long time, until a friend **cleared up** our disagreement.
No nurse could understand the doctor's point until he **cleared** it **up.**

7. **to put off**—to postpone, to delay, to defer

Usual subjects: people
Usual objects: matter, decision; meeting, appointment, conference

I want to think over this matter fully, so I'll **put** my decision **off** until next week.
We had to **put off** the meeting because many members could not show up at that time.

The businessman hadn't gotten over his cold so he had to **put off** his appointment with the company president.

8. **to carry out**—to fulfill, to accomplish

   Usual subjects: people
   Usual objects: promise, obligation, responsibility; job, duty
   This idiom is very close in meaning to **to live up to.**

   He **carried out** all his promises so everyone looked up to him.
   To try for a promotion, the office worker **carried out** his responsibilities carefully and thoroughly.
   If you want your work to be respected, you have to **carry** it **out** well.

9. **to bring about**—to cause (to happen)

   Usual subjects: people; *situation* (circumstances, plan, problem, etc.)
   Usual objects: *situation* (change, accident, illness, etc.)
   This idiom is used when someone or something (subject) is the reason why a situation occurred. It is close in meaning to **to come about.**

   The new chairman **brought about** a big change in his company's organizational structure.
   The bicyclist **brought about** an accident when he suddenly crossed the street in front of a car.
   What **brought about** John's illness? I thought he was taking care of himself.

10. **to call off**—to cancel, to stop

    Usual subjects: people
    Usual objects: meeting, conference; *project* (plan, proposal, deal); *travel* (trip, journey, expedition); marriage, wedding

    We had to **call** the meeting **off** because the chairman was out-of-town.
    When his wife didn't get over her illness, Mr. Smith **called off** their trip to Europe.
    Bob and Ann **called off** their wedding because they couldn't clear up their differences of opinion.

11. **to look up**—to try to find, to search for

    Usual subjects: people
    Usual objects: *information* (fact, detail, word; address; numbers); people

    He **looked up** the necessary facts in the law book.

Students use dictionaries in order to **look up** vocabulary definitions.

When I visited New York, I **looked up** my old high school friend who lives there.

12. **to point out**—to explain; to indicate

Usual subjects: people
Usual objects: aspect, truth, fact; law; argument

The teacher **pointed out** other facts which had been left out of the discussion.

The policeman **pointed out** several driving laws I had violated.

The lawyer **pointed out** some arguments which brought up doubt about the man's innocence.

13. **to talk over**—to discuss (fully); to consider

Usual subjects: people
Usual objects: matter, problem, question; project, plan; things

The principal **talked over** the student problem with the teacher.

The corporation members **talked** the plan **over** for some time.

To clear up a marital problem, husband and wife should **talk** things **over.**

14. **to make out**—1) to distinguish, to manage to see
    2) to complete, to fill out (a form)

#1 Usual subjects: people
   Usual objects: *things which are hard to see* (figure, shape, cars in fog)

   It was very foggy so it was hard to **make out** the figures of people walking on the side of the road.

   In the distance I could **make out** the outlines of cows walking on top of a hill.

#2 Usual subjects: people
   Usual objects: application, form, questionnaire; check, order

   The bank looked up his account number so that he could **make out** the check request form correctly.

   To apply for a credit card, you have to **make out** this application form.

15. **to take off**—1) to remove
    2) to have free time off

#1 Usual subjects: people
   Usual objects: coat, hat, clothes

   When my guests showed up, they entered and **took off** their coats.
   I like to **take off** my shoes when I'm at home.

#2 Usual subjects: people
   Usual objects: *period of time* (day, week, month); holiday, vacation

   I had gone without a vacation for too long, so finally I **took** two weeks **off.**
   He **took off** the summer to write a new novel.

Class discussion:

Now that you have learned the meanings of the idioms and how to use them in sentences, go back to **Exercise I** and **Exercise II** and check your answers. As you do this, consider the following questions:

1. How many idioms did you guess correctly in **Exercise I?**

2. How much better did you do in **Exercise II?**

3. Are there any idiom meanings which are still not clear to you?

4. Is there anything you have noticed about the grammatical usage of these idioms?

IV. LEARNING THE GRAMMAR RULES

Part A   All of the idioms in this chapter are composed of a *transitive verb + movable particle.* The verb is transitive because a noun phrase must be used as an object.

Example:

transitive verb + movable particle: **to clear up**

The president	cleared up	the problem
subject	verbal idiom	object

1. Are the transitive verb and particle connected in:
   a) meaning b) grammar c) both meaning and grammar?

2. In the preceding section, did you discover another place to put the particle? Where?

Part B Look carefully at the following sets of sentences. Some are correct and some are incorrect (*). Answer the questions by comparing the sentences.

Set 1

1. The president cleared up the problem carefully.
2. *The president cleared carefully up the problem.
3. The president cleared the problem up carefully.
4. *The president cleared up carefully the problem.
5. The president carefully cleared up the problem.

a. What is the difference between sentences #1 and #3?

b. Fill in the appropriate answers:

With the idioms in this chapter, the _____ may

be placed before or after the _____ .

c. Which sentence is another correct form of #1 and #3?

d. Where is it *wrong* to place an adverb?

With the idioms in this chapter, the particle may be placed on either side of the object, but not anywhere else in the sentence. An adverb may *not* be placed between the verb + particle or between the particle and object because the verb + particle are connected in both meaning and grammar.

The president cleared *up* the problem carefully.	(correct position)
The president cleared the problem *up* carefully.	(correct position)
The president *carefully* cleared up the problem.	(correct position)
*The president cleared *carefully* up the problem.	(incorrect position)
*The president cleared *carefully* the problem up.	(incorrect position)

Set 2

1. The president cleared up the problem.
2. *The president cleared up it.
3. The lawyer stuck to his argument.

4. The lawyer stuck to it.
5. The president cleared it up.
6. *The lawyer stuck it to.

a. What is the difference between the idioms in sentences #1 and #3?

b. Circle the correct answers:

   1. In the idiom **clear up,** *up* is a (particle or preposition).

   2. In the idiom **stick to,** *to* is a (particle or preposition).

c. Which sentence is the correct form of #2?

d. Which sentence is the correct form of #6?

e. Compare sentences #4 and #5. What can you say about the use of pronouns with transitive verbs and particles?

You must be very careful not to confuse the grammar of intransitive verbs with prepositions, and transitive verbs with particles.

Compare:

a. *Transitive verb with particle*
   I held the meeting *up.*   (particle can be placed
   I held *up* the meeting.   before or after object)
   *I held *stubbornly* up the   (impossible position)
   meeting

b. *Intransitive verb with preposition*
   I stuck *to* my opinion.   (preposition can only be
   *I stuck my opinion *to.*   placed before noun phrase)
   I stuck *firmly* to my   (possible position)
   opinion.

The general rule for pronouns is that they always *precede* particles, but always *follow* prepositions.

Particle:

The president cleared *it* up.   (correct position)
*The president cleared up *it.*   (incorrect position)

Preposition:

The lawyer stuck to *it.*   (correct position)
*The lawyer stuck *it* to.   (incorrect position)

V. MULTIPLE-CHOICE EXERCISE

Choose the idiom from this chapter, or a previous one, which has the best meaning in the context below. No idiom is used twice as a correct answer. Be very careful about the grammar rules which you have learned.

1. Do you ever fail to do your duties or do you always _____ _____ them?
   - a. believe in
   - b. live up to
   - c. carry out

2. When the noise _____ , I began to speak.
   - a. broke in
   - b. went without
   - c. died down

3. I tried to get through to him, but I couldn't _____ _____ his misunderstanding.
   - a. work up to
   - b. catch on
   - c. clear up

4. I hated to _____ my stereo, but I had to sell it to stick to my budget.
   - a. part with
   - b. did without
   - c. go through

5. When you _____ _____ your home life, can you look up to your parents for the way they raised you?
   - a. look out for
   - b. go into
   - c. look back on

6. It took many years for me to _____ an important position in my company.
   - a. keep up with
   - b. work up to
   - c. settle down

7. Did your committee _____ _____ the problem carefully before deciding on it?
   - a. get over
   - b. talk over
   - c. touch on

8. Although he _____ the best job available, he only worked up to assistant.
   - a. part with
   - b. get ahead
   - c. tried for

9. The soldiers stopped fighting and just _____ as the planes dropped bombs on the enemy ahead.
   - a. broke in
   - b. tried out
   - c. looked on

10. The teacher is reading his lecture too quickly so I can't _____ his ideas.
    - a. catch on
    - b. keep up with
    - c. hold on

11. There's too much noise here for me to study; I can't _____ _____ it.

　　a. go through
　　b. think over
　　c. put up with

12. Did the policeman _____ the mistake you made?

　　a. point out
　　b. take off
　　c. make up

VI. WRITING EXERCISE

Answer each question by using the idiom in a meaningful, grammatical sentence.

1. Why do some people make up excuses for their mistakes?

2. Why would the President think over an important problem before making a decision?

3. If you had children, how would you bring them up?

4. What kinds of gifts do T.V. game shows give away?

5. Why do people try things out before they buy them?

6. How can a teacher clear up a student's mistake?

7. What was the most recent task which you put off?

8. Why should students carry out their assignments completely?

9. What problems might bring a revolution about?

10. For what reason would you have to call off a party?

11. Where would you look up the location of a city?

12. Who do you talk over your problems with?

13. In a hospital, who can point out the cause of your illness?

14. When is it difficult to make a traffic sign out?

15. When is the next time that you can take off a week or more from school?

6

Transitive Verbs with Immovable Particles

Type A

to lead on   to fill in
to do over   to tie down
to tell apart   to kick around
to see off

Type B

to make up   to give up
to take up   to give off
to put forth   to find out
to carry on

I. GUESSING THE MEANING FROM CONTEXT

Guess the meaning of each idiom as it is used in the following sentences. Provide either a one-word synonym or a definition. Underline the context clues as you are trying to guess the meaning.

1. If you believe in telling the truth, you should never **lead** someone **on.** _____

2. Your homework is poor; please review the instructions and **do** your homework **over** for next week. _____

3. Joe's twin brother takes after Joe in personality and behavior, as well as appearance, so Joe's wife often can't **tell** them **apart.** _____

4. Tom's parents were taking off a week for a trip, so he went to the airport to **see** them **off.** _____

5. My assistant was not too familiar with the details of the new plan, so I **filled** him **in** during our conference. _____

6. Now I can't go to parties every night like I used to because my job and my family really **tie** me **down.** _____

7. Before we talk over the plan with the president, **kick** it **around** for a while with your assistants whenever you have some time. _____

8. Fifty states, including Alaska and Hawaii, **make up** the United States. _____

9. After we finished Lesson 1, we **took up** Lesson 3 instead of **taking up** Lesson 2. _____

10. At first, the lazy student almost gave up but eventually he **put forth** greater effort. _____

11. The chairman and his assistants **carried on** their meeting in the restaurant because they couldn't hold it in the conference room. _____

12. His physical health was so poor that he had to **give up** smoking and drinking. _____

13. A skunk is a small black animal, with a white stripe down its back, which **gives off** a terrible smell. _____

14. When you looked into the matter in the library, did you **find out** any answers? _____

Class discussion:

Decide which idioms were easy to guess and which were difficult. Discuss the importance of context clues in your decisions.

II. DEFINITION CORRESPONDENCE

Using **Exercise I** to help you, check your guesses by choosing the correct idiom which corresponds to the definition you see on the left side. Be sure to use context clues and to use the correct grammar forms.

Type A

to lead on	to fill in
to do over	to tie down
to tell apart	to kick around
to see off	

Type B

to make up	to give up
to take up	to give off
to put forth	to find out
to carry on	

(to inform)   1. Because he wasn't in on the conference where we discussed the new laws, I _____ him _____.

(to distinguish between)   2. Because I am color-blind, I can't _____ colors _____.

(to deceive)   3. He _____ Mary _____ about loving her, but he really couldn't put up with the idea of marrying her.

(to repeat)

4. Because I wasn't satisfied with the quality of the work, I _____ it _____ so that it was better.

(to restrict)

5. Tom's job _____ him _____ all day, so he can only stop by to visit us in the evenings.

(to say goodbye)

6. When your guests leave, it's polite to _____ them _____ at the front door.

(to discuss informally)

7. Let's _____ this idea _____ before we talk it over more carefully at the meeting.

(to begin work on)

8. In class we _____ a study of idioms after we went over the vocabulary we had learned.

(to discover)

9. When are you going to _____ the solution to the problem?

(to produce)

10. Workers who _____ good work will receive more money.

(to hold)

11. Do you want to hold the business meeting in the hotel, or will you _____ your business somewhere else?

(to form)

12. It's much easier to teach when only ten students _____ a class.

(to stop a bad habit)

13. The bachelor _____ going to parties every night because he was going through his money too quickly.

(to release)

14. Pollution in a river will cause the water to _____ a bad odor.

III. EXPLANATION OF THE IDIOMS

1. **to lead** (someone) **on**—to deceive, to mislead

   Usual subjects: people; advertisement, TV commercial
   Usual objects: people
   This idiom means that the subject makes someone believe something which is not really true.

   The salesman **led** me **on** about the quality of the product so that I would buy it.
   Used car dealers often **lead** people **on** to buy cars which soon break down.

2. **to do** (something) **over**—1) to repeat, to do again
   2) to redecorate

   #1 Usual subjects: people
   Usual objects: assignment, homework; job, work

   The student's homework was so bad that I told him to **do** it **over.**
   The secretary did the work poorly, so her boss told her to **do** it **over.**

   #2 Usual subjects: people, company, redecorator
   Usual objects: house, room, office, someone's place

   We had to **do** the kitchen **over** after the small fire made the walls black.
   The redecorating company **did** my whole house **over.**

3. **to tell** (people/things) **apart**—to distinguish between two or more similar people or things

   Usual subjects: people
   Usual objects: *people* (brothers/sisters, twins); two similar things

   Tom and Jim look so much alike that I can't **tell** them **apart.**
   Most new cars look so similar that it's impossible to **tell** them **apart.**

4. **to see** (someone) **off**—to say goodbye (upon someone's departure)

   Usual subjects: *people* (family, friends)
   Usual objects: people
   This idiom is used when someone says goodbye to someone who is leaving (usually on a trip) for a period of time.

   Tom's parents **saw** him **off** at the airport when he left home to try for a job in Europe.

Wives used to **see** their husbands **off** to work at the front door, but this is no longer common.

We **saw** John and Sally **off** at the harbor when they went on a cruise.

5. **to fill** (someone) **in**—to inform, to give more complete information

Usual subjects: people
Usual objects: people

If the new employee doesn't know about his duties, **fill** him **in.**

The President can't go without current information, so his advisors frequently **fill** him **in** on daily events.

6. **to tie** (someone) **down**—to limit or restrict one's freedom to do something

Usual subjects: job, work; family, children, pets; illness
Usual objects: people

He'd like to part with some of his duties because his present job **ties** him **down** twelve hours a day.

Many parents don't get around freely because their children **tie** them **down.**

Tom's serious illness **tied** him **down** in the hospital for three weeks.

7. **to kick** (something) **around**—to discuss or consider informally

Usual subjects: people
Usual objects: plan, idea, suggestion, proposal

After we **kicked** the plan **around** for several days, we were able to clear up the remaining difficulties.

Don't just **kick** his proposal **around;** go into it more deeply.

8. **to make up**—to form, to compose, to constitute

Usual subjects: a plural noun
Usual objects: a singular noun
This idiom is used when a number of things together form a single unit.

How many words **make up** this sentence?
Five singers **make up** that rock-and-roll group.

9. **to take up**—to begin work on; to start as a hobby or sport

Usual subjects: people
Usual objects: *subject of study* (languages, biology, medicine, etc.); *hobbies/sports* (reading, gardening; golf, tennis)

More American students should **take up** a foreign language and follow it through until they know it well.

Because he went in for exercising, he **took up** jogging.

Rich people can afford to **take up** whatever hobbies they like.

10. **to put forth**—1) to produce, to show, to display
                     2) to propose, to suggest (strongly)

   #1 Usual subjects: people
      Usual objects: energy, work, effort, strength

      Students who **put forth** much effort will get ahead.
      In the contest, our team was trying for the prize, so we **put forth** a lot of effort.

   #2 Usual subjects: people
      Usual objects: suggestion, proposal, idea, plan; argument

      The President **put forth** his best plan for cutting down on inflation.
      The lawyer **put forth** a strong argument against the defendant.

11. **to carry on**—to conduct, to hold

   Usual subjects: people; committee, class
   Usual objects: conversation, discussion, talk, meeting, conference

   We **carried on** a conversation for two hours because she felt like opening up completely.
   The student council **carried on** its meeting in the bar, not the conference room!
   In her absence, the manager asked her assistant to **carry on** the work.

12. **to give up**—to stop (a bad habit)

   Usual subjects: people
   Usual objects: *bad habit* (smoking, drinking, wasting time)

   If everyone **gave up** smoking and drinking, this would bring about the breakdown of the tobacco and liquor industries.
   You should **give up** driving too fast in your sports car, or you'll have an accident.

13. **to give off**—to release, to emit or produce (a bad smell or smoke)

   Usual subjects: people, animals; bad-smelling things; fire
   Usual objects: smell, odor, stink, aroma; smoke

If you don't shower more often, your body will **give off** an unpleasant odor.

Week-old garbage usually **gives off** a terrible stink.

The small oven fire **gave off** much smoke, which ruined the walls, so we had to do the kitchen over.

14. **to find out**—to discover, to learn by investigation

Usual subjects: people
Usual objects: some unknown fact or situation

Did you ever **find out** the answer to the crossword puzzle?

I'd like to **find out** why he wants to get back at me; I didn't lead him on about anything!

Mary **found out** about the surprise party even though we tried to keep it a secret.

Class discussion:

Now that you have learned the meanings of the idioms and how to use them in sentences, go back to **Exercise I** and **Exercise II** and check your answers. As you do this, consider the following questions:

1. How many idioms did you guess correctly in **Exercise I?**

2. How much better did you do in **Exercise II?**

3. Are there any idiom meanings which are still not clear to you?

4. Is there anything you have noticed about the grammatical usage of these idioms?

IV. LEARNING THE GRAMMAR RULES

Part A   All of the idioms in this chapter are composed of a *transitive verb + immovable particle*. The verb is transitive because a noun phrase is used as an object. In this case, however, there are two different types of verbal idiom.

Examples:

transitive verb + immovable particle (Type A): **to kick around**

My friends kicked my suggestion around.
subject — object — verbal idiom

transitive verb + immovable particle (Type B): **to make up**

Five rooms make up this house.

subject   verbal idiom   object

1. How are the transitive verb and particle connected?

2. What is the difference between the two types of idioms?

3. How do the idioms in this chapter differ from the idioms in the previous chapter?

Part B   Look carefully at the following sentences. Some are correct and some are incorrect (*). Answer the questions by comparing the sentences.

Set 1

1. I can tell the twins apart easily.
2. *I can tell apart the twins easily.
3. I can easily tell the twins apart.
4. *I can tell easily the twins apart.
5. *I can tell the twins easily apart.

a. What is the difference between sentences #1 and #2?

b. Which sentences are correct forms of #4 and #5?

c. Why is the adverb in the wrong position in sentences #4 and #5?

With some of the idioms in this chapter, the particle may only be placed *after* the object. The verb and particle are connected in both meaning and grammar, so an adverb cannot be placed anywhere between them.

I can tell the twins apart *easily*.   (correct position)
I can *easily* tell the twins apart.   (correct position)
*I can tell *easily* the twins apart.   (incorrect position)
*I can tell the twins *easily* apart.   (incorrect position)

Set 2

1. The student found out the answer quickly.
2. *The student found the answer out quickly.
3. The student quickly found out the answer.

4. *The student found quickly out the answer.
5. The student found it out quickly.
6. *The student found out it quickly.

a. What is the difference between sentences #1 and #2?

b. Which sentences are correct forms of #4?

c. Where is it *wrong* to place an adverb?

d. Where should a pronoun object be placed?

With some of the idioms in this chapter, the particle may only be placed *before* the object. However, when a pronoun object is used, the particle can only be placed after it (see **Chapter 5**).

The student found *out* the answer quickly.   (correct position)
*The student found the answer *out* quickly.   (incorrect position)
The student found *it* out quickly.   (correct position)
*The student found out *it* quickly.   (incorrect position)

The verb and particle are again connected in meaning and grammar, so an adverb may not be placed between them.

The student found out the answer *quickly*.   (correct position)
The student *quickly* found out the answer.   (correct position)
*The student found *quickly* out the answer.   (incorrect position)
*The student found out *quickly* the answer.   (incorrect position)

Part C Choose the appropriate grammatical description for each idiom from **Chapters 5** and **6.** Also write a sentence below each idiom, using the correct grammatical form.

  I. Verb with Movable Particle

 II. Verb with Immovable Particle after Object (Type A)

III. Verb with Immovable Particle before Object (Type B)

a. **to lead on** _____

   sentence: _____

b. **to think over** _____

   sentence: _____

c. **to find out** _____

    sentence: _____

V. MULTIPLE-CHOICE EXERCISE

Choose the idiom from this chapter, or a previous one, which has the best meaning in the context below. No idiom is used twice as a correct answer. Be _very_ careful about the grammar rules which you have learned; some choices may be incorrect because of the grammar rules.

1. I asked him to go to the research center to _____ some information _____ for me.
   a. find . . . out
   b. look . . . up
   c. make . . . up

2. If you put off your work, you can't _____ it _____ .
   a. kick . . . around
   b. point . . . out
   c. carry . . . out

3. During high school Tom _____ bad friends, but in college he made better friends.
   a. looked out for
   b. looked up
   c. ran around with

4. I can't _____ him because he always breaks in loudly while other people are talking.
   a. do away with
   b. put up with
   c. try for

5. He almost wanted to give up, but I told him to _____ more effort.
   a. settle down
   b. keep up with
   c. put forth

6. A big traffic jam came about when a drunk driver _____ an accident.
   a. looked out for
   b. brought about
   c. brought up

7. Why did they _____ their talk in the kitchen instead of the living room?
   a. kick around
   b. carry on
   c. point out

8. A serious illness will always _____ someone _____ in bed.
   a. keep . . . up
   b. hold . . . on
   c. tie . . . down

9. If you have any questions, please _____ them _____ now.
   a. come . . . up with
   b. hold . . . back
   c. bring . . . up

10. When the noise died down, the professor _____

    _____ the next subject of discussion with the students.

    a. filled in
    b. got ahead
    c. took up

11. The little children in his kindergarten class refused to

    _____ .

    a. settle down
    b. live up to
    c. do over

12. I understand the first three grammar rules, but please

    _____ the last rule for me again briefly.

    a. fill in
    b. touch on
    c. get through to

VI. WRITING EXERCISE

Please answer each question or statement by using the idiom in a meaningful, grammatical sentence.

1. Why is it bad to lead someone on?

2. When should a secretary do her work over?

3. In what parts of the world is it hard to tell day and night apart?

4. When was the last time that you saw someone off at the train station?

5. When a student has been absent, why should a teacher fill him in on the classwork?

6. What responsibilities tie you down?

7. Why is it important to kick an idea around before making a final decision?

8. How many meters make up a kilometer?

9. After you finish school, what work do you want to take up?

10. Why should a new student put forth his best effort?

11. Where would you carry on a picnic for many people?

12. What personal habit would you like to give up?

13. Name two things which give off a bad smell.

14. Where can you find out the meaning of an unfamiliar vocabulary word?

7

Transitive Verbs with Prepositions (Type I)

to hold against	to engage in
to leave to	to confuse with
to lend to	to devote to
to put through	to put above
to draw from	to pull through

I. GUESSING THE MEANING FROM CONTEXT

Guess the meaning of each idiom as it is used in the following sentences. Provide either a one-word synonym or a definition. Underline the context clues as you are trying to guess the meaning. These are difficult idioms to guess, so please just do your best.

1. He tried hard to get ahead, so I can't **hold** his failure **against** him. _____

2. You've been responsible for enough of the work; **leave** the remaining work **to** your assistant. _____

3. The support of other scientists **lends** strength **to** the scientist's new theory. _____

4. Ten U.S. Senators helped to **put** the bill **through** Congress; the President was very grateful for this special support. _____

5. The successful student **drew** pleasure **from** the fact that he had passed all his exams. _____

6. My talkative friend called me up and **engaged** me **in** a long, boring conversation. _____

7. I **confuse** Jim **with** Mike because I can't tell them apart. _____

8. The kind doctor **devoted** his whole life **to** helping poor people; thousands turned to him for help. _____

9. I **put** freedom **above** money because, without freedom, money doesn't mean anything. _____

10. When the alcoholic was considering suicide, the helpful psychiatrist **pulled** him **through** this difficult period. _____

Class discussion:

Decide which idioms were more difficult to guess than others. Discuss the importance of context clues in your decisions.

II. DEFINITION CORRESPONDENCE

Using **Exercise I** to help you, check your guesses by choosing the correct idiom which corresponds to the definition you see on the left side. Be sure to use context clues and to use the correct grammar forms.

to hold against	to engage in
to leave to	to confuse with
to lend to	to devote to
to put through	to put above
to draw from	to pull through

(to cause to pass)

1. The chairman successfully _____ the proposal _____ the committee by putting forth his best arguments.

(to make important)

2. The research you did for me definitely _____ more support _____ my new theory.

(to regard as more important than)

3. When you're very tired, it's better to _____ sleep _____ work, or you'll get sick.

(to obtain from)

4. Despite my illness, I _____ comfort _____ the fact that I had two fine nurses caring for me.

(to help to get over)

5. When Joe had trouble getting over the death of his wife, his friends _____ him _____ this difficult time.

(to make responsible for)

6. You could cut down on your responsibilities if you _____ _____ more work _____ your secretary; that's her job.

(to make much effort in)

7. The U.S. President should expect to _____ all his hours _____ taking care of government business; it's really a full-time job.

(to fail to tell apart)

8. I always _____ this word _____ that word because they're almost spelled the same way.

(to blame on)

9. Pollution is now very serious; I _____ this situation _____ careless corporations that get rid of their wastes improperly.

(to make occupied)

10. When Peter ran across me after many years, he _____ me _____ a long conversation.

III. EXPLANATION OF THE IDIOMS

1. **to hold against**—to blame on, to put the blame on

   Usual subjects: people
   Usual objects: it; failure, shortcomings; a grudge
   Usual NPs: people
   When *it* is used, a *that-clause* will follow the NP to explain it.

   I **hold** it **against** him that he refused to help me.
   Do you **hold** it **against** Mary that she divorced you?
   I can **hold** his failure **against** him because he never tried for a passing grade.
   Why do you **hold** a grudge **against** him?

2. **to leave to**—to make responsible for, to leave in charge of

   Usual subjects: people
   Usual objects: work, arrangements; everything, it all, things
   Usual NPs: people

   The president **left** the conference arrangements **to** his assistant.

Don't **leave** everything **to** him; you should help out too!

If you **leave** it all **to** me, I promise that I'll carry it out well.

3. **to lend to**—to make important, to make believable

Usual subjects: support, help, backing; proof, facts, research

Usual objects: importance, significance, credence, meaning

Usual NPs: view, theory, analysis, belief, idea

The support of the government **lent** importance **to** the new economic theory of marketing control.

The laboratory research will **lend** significance **to** the police analysis of the crime.

Proof of outer space people would **lend** credence **to** a belief in UFO's.

4. **to put through**—to cause to pass or succeed

Usual subjects: people

Usual objects: people, oneself; bill, measure, proposed law

Usual NPs: school, university, college; Congress, Senate, legislature

This idiom is very common when: 1) a student is supported or supports himself in college or 2) a politician or group succeeds in getting support for a law.

Joe was lucky that his parents **put** him **through** college.

Mike wasn't so lucky because he had to **put** himself **through** university.

The lobby against pollution helped to **put** an air-quality control bill **through** Congress.

5. **to draw from**—to obtain from, to get from

Usual subjects: people

Usual objects: pleasure, comfort; relief, consolation

Usual NPs: knowledge, thought, realization, fact

The NP is usually explained further in a following *that-clause*.

The retiring chairman **drew** pleasure **from** the knowledge that he had put forth his best effort.

When the student was refused by Harvard University, he **drew** consolation **from** the fact that hundreds of other students were also not accepted.

6. **to engage in**—to make busy, to make occupied

Usual subjects: people

Usual objects: people, oneself

Usual NPs: some activity

The employer **engaged** his new workers **in** hard labor.
The diligent student **engaged** himself **in** concentrated study.
The car salesman **engaged** me **in** a long conversation about why he put Chevrolets above Fords.

7. **to confuse with**—to fail to tell apart

Usual subjects: people
Usual objects: people; real, genuine, or authentic product
Usual NPs; people; fake or imitation product

It's hard to tell the Smith twins apart, so people often **confuse** one brother **with** the other.
I **confused** a similar car **with** mine in the parking lot.

8. **to devote to**—to make much effort in, to dedicate oneself to

Usual subject: people
Usual objects: oneself; time, thought, effort, attention, energy
Usual NPs: a worthwhile purpose or activity (often a *Verb + ing* form)

The young doctor **devoted** himself **to** helping the poor and sick.
The athlete **devoted** much energy **to** getting ahead in his sport.
The teacher **devoted** much time **to** going over the vocabulary.

9. **to put above**—to regard as more important than

Usual subjects: people
Usual objects: something important (to the subject)
Usual NPs: something less important; all else, everything else

If you lead someone on, you **put** self-interest **above** truth.
He quit his job to go with her to Europe because he **puts** his love for her **above** his work.
A good husband and wife who want to succeed will **put** their marriage **above** all else.

10. **to pull through**—to help to get over, to assist in recovery

Usual subjects: *people* (doctor, family, friend); government
Usual objects: *people* (patient, family member); country
Usual NPs: sickness, illness; difficult period, hard times, emergency

The competent doctors **pulled** the patient **through** his serious illness by giving him the best possible attention.

Tom's family **pulled** him **through** the difficult period following his wife's death.

The weak government leaned on the U.S. to **pull** the country **through** the emergency.

Class discussion:

Now that you have learned the meanings of the idioms and how to use them in sentences, go back to **Exercise I** and **Exercise II** and check your answers. As you do this, consider the following questions:

1. How many idioms did you guess correctly in **Exercise I?**

2. How much better did you do in **Exercise II?**

3. Are there any idiom meanings which are still not clear to you?

4. Is there anything you have noticed about the grammatical usage of these idioms?

IV. LEARNING THE GRAMMAR RULES

Part A All of the idioms in this chapter are composed of a *transitive verb + preposition*. The transitive verb will be followed by an object, and the preposition will be followed by a noun phrase.

Example:

transitive verb + preposition: **to devote to**

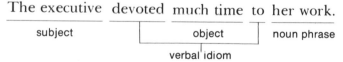

1. Is the preposition connected to the verb in:
   a) meaning b) grammar c) both meaning and grammar?

   How did you decide?

2. Do you think that the preposition may be placed before the object? Why or why not?

Part B Look at the following set of sentences. Some sentences are correct and some are incorrect (*). Answer the questions by comparing the sentences.

1. The president left the work to his secretary.
2. *The president left to the work his secretary.
3. The senator put the bill through Congress.
4. *The senator put the bill Congress through.

a. What is the difference between sentences #1 and #2?

b. How does sentence #3 differ from sentence #4?

c. Fill in the appropriate answers:

    1. An _____ always follows a transitive

    _____ .

    2. A _____ always precedes a _____ .

A preposition may not be placed before the object because the preposition is connected to the following noun phrase in grammar. The preposition introduces the prepositional phrase, so it may not be placed after the noun phrase.

The president left the work *to* his secretary. (correct position)
*The president left *to* the work his secretary. (incorrect position)
The senator put the bill *through* Congress. (correct position)
*The senator put the bill Congress *through*. (incorrect position)

You learned in **Chapter 2** that a manner adverb can be placed between a verb and preposition. However, it is unusual for an adverb to precede the prepositions in these idioms because an object follows the transitive verb. The normal position for adverbs is at the end of the sentence, although manner adverbs ending in *-ly* are often put before the verb.

The senator put the bill through Congress *quickly*. (correct)
The senator *quickly* put the bill through Congress. (correct)
The senator put the bill through Congress *last year*. (correct)
*The senator *last year* put the bill through Congress. (incorrect)
†The senator put the bill *quickly* through Congress. (unusual)

(†unusual)

V. MULTIPLE-CHOICE EXERCISE

Choose the idiom from this chapter, or a previous one, which has the best meaning in the context below. No idiom is used twice as a correct answer. Be very careful about the grammar rules which you have learned.

1. After you left France, did you _____ French in

   school?

   a. take up
   b. do over
   c. engage in

2. Color-blind people _____ green _____

   _____ blue.

   a. tell . . . apart
   b. put . . . above
   c. confuse . . . with

3. If you fail the first time, _____ it _____

   _____ .

   a. put . . . through
   b. do . . . over
   c. put . . . above

4. How can I _____ if you don't go into it care-

   fully?

   a. catch on
   b. talk over
   c. engage in

5. I try to _____ two hours every night _____

   _____ my school work.

   a. put . . . above
   b. devote . . . to
   c. leave . . . to

6. A four-foot person _____ anywhere he goes.

   a. turns to
   b. stands out
   c. goes without

7. How can you _____ $10,000 in one week?

   a. cut down on
   b. go through
   c. lend to

8. A close friend helped to _____ John _____

   _____ his emotional crisis.

   a. engage . . . in
   b. pull . . . through
   c. draw . . . from

9. He looks so familiar; who does he _____ ?

   a. confuse with
   b. take after
   c. give off

10. I hadn't practiced the piano for three weeks, so I _____

    _____ my songs.

   a. came to
   b. brushed up on
   c. took off

11. This book carefully _____ the subject of poverty in the Third World.

a. goes into
b. touches on
c. turns to

12. The parents didn't like yardwork so they _____ _____ it _____ their sons.

a. drew . . . from
b. left . . . to
c. filled . . . in

VI. WRITING EXERCISE

Please answer each question by using the idiom in a meaningful, grammatical sentence.

1. What would you hold against a criminal?

2. Why is it unfair to leave everything to only one person?

3. How do you lend meaning to an idea you have?

4. Who is putting you through school?

5. Do you draw pleasure from the fact that you're learning English? Why?

6. What hobbies do you like to engage in?

7. If you saw a bright light in the sky, what could you confuse it with?

8. What, if anything, do you like to devote yourself to?

9. What do you put above your own interests?

10. When you have troubles, who helps to pull you through your problems?

8

Transitive Verbs with Prepositions (Type II)

to take advantage of	to make sense of
to lose track of	to take exception to
to keep an eye on	to find fault with
to take a stand on	to make light of
to make a point of	to take charge of

I. GUESSING THE MEANING FROM CONTEXT

Guess the meaning of each idiom as it is used in the following sentences. Provide either a one-word synonym or a definition. Underline the context clues as you are trying to guess the meaning.

1. If you have an American roommate, **take advantage of** him for carrying on conversations and answering questions. _____

2. I've **lost track of** my wallet; can you help me locate it? _____

3. While her mother went to the store, Mary **kept an eye on** the children playing outside. _____

4. At first Joe couldn't come up with a decision about our problem, but finally he **took a stand on** it. _____

5. Because I was late to class, I **made a point of** apologizing to the teacher after class; she appreciated my concern. _____

6. Even though the speaker had a strong accent, Harry could catch on to his story, but Tom couldn't **make sense of** it at all. _____

7. Everyone voted in the same way except Joe; he **took exception to** our vote. _____

8. The teacher **found fault with** the student because he didn't do his homework and often slept in class. _____

9. Most people think that marriage is important, but happy bachelors would laugh and **make light of** it. _____

10. If you leave the business to your efficient assistant, he'll **take charge of** it and do a fine job. _____

Class discussion:

Decide which idioms were easy to guess and which were difficult. Consider the importance of context clues in your decisions.

II. DEFINITION CORRESPONDENCE

Using **Exercise I** to help you, check your guesses by choosing the correct idiom which corresponds to the definition you see on the left side. Be sure to use context clues and to use the correct grammar forms.

to take advantage of	to make sense of
to lose track of	to take exception to
to keep an eye on	to find fault with
to take a stand on	to make light of
to make a point of	to take charge of

(to consider unimportant)

1. I thought the problem was rather serious, but my friend _____ it.

(to make a firm decision on)

2. Before you _____ anything, you should think it over carefully.

(to use for personal benefit)

3. The clever son _____ his parents to put him through college and to buy him a car.

(to assume responsibility for)

4. Because the previous president had given up and left the company, the vice-president _____ it.

(to watch carefully)

5. The old lady didn't _____ her dog so unfortunately it ran away.

(to criticize strongly)

6. If someone doesn't live up to his duties and gives up very easily, it is fair to _____ him.

(to disagree with)	7. I _____ your plan; I think we should do it my way.
(to be careful to)	8. I _____ thanking my friend for the wonderful gift she had given me.
(to misplace)	9. Bob had to borrow a pencil from his friend because he had _____ his own.
(to understand)	10. The movie was so strange and disorganized that I couldn't _____ it.

III. EXPLANATION OF THE IDIOMS

1. **to take advantage of**—to use for one's personal benefit

   Usual subjects: people
   Usual NPs: a beneficial situation or condition; people
   This idiom can have the negative meaning of "to use someone unfairly" when the NP is a person; the context will
   help you decide if the meaning is positive or negative.

   He **took advantage of** the summer vacation period to travel
   around the United States.
   During the summer, tourists **took advantage of** the good
   weather to lie on the beaches.
   Students should **take advantage of** their teachers to get answers to their questions.   (positive meaning)
   He **takes advantage of** his fine secretary by leaving all the
   work to her and doing nothing himself; I wouldn't put up
   with him!   (negative meaning)

2. **to lose track of**—1) to be unable to find, to misplace, not to
   know the location of
   2) not to know what time it is

   #1 Usual subjects: people
   Usual NPs: people; things; idea, argument, what someone said

   Although I ran across one high school friend last
   month, I've **lost track of** all my other old friends.
   She **lost track of** her umbrella at the office, so she borrowed her friend's.
   I was so bored that I **lost track of** what he was saying.

#2 Usual subjects: people
    Usual objects: the time, time of day

Tom's work was so interesting that he **lost track of** the time.

I've been so busy! I've **lost track of** the time of day!

I'm sorry I'm late for our appointment. I **lost track of** the time.

3. **to keep an eye on**—to take care of, to watch carefully, to guard

Usual subjects: *people* (mother, grandmother, babysitter, soldier, etc.)
Usual NPs: children, animals; house, an important thing

The dog got away with the steaks because we didn't **keep an eye on** it!

Always **keep an eye on** small children playing near busy streets.

Could you **keep an eye on** our house while we take a week off for a small trip?

The bank guard **kept an eye on** the parking lot while they were loading the armored truck with money.

4. **to take a stand on**—to make a firm decision, to hold a strong opinion

Usual subjects: people
Usual NPs: situation, problem, matter, issue

The lazy man didn't want to deal with the problem, so he refused to **take a stand on** it.

The American people expect the President to **take a stand on** every important national issue.

Since he wasn't in on the discussion of the matter, he couldn't honestly **take a stand on** it.

5. **to make a point of**—to be careful to, to be sure to, to take pains to

Usual subjects: people
Usual NPs: doing something
The NP usually starts with a *verb + ing* form.

Punctual people always **make a point of** being a little early.

If someone sends you a gift, **make a point of** thanking them the next time you meet.

Since she couldn't put up with him at all, she **made a point of** ignoring him altogether.

6. **to make sense of**—to understand, to interpret successfully

Usual subjects: people
Usual NPs: idea, plan; conversation, speech, discussion; language

I can't **make sense of** his plan to take up elephant hunting!
The telephone connection was so bad that the operator couldn't **make sense of** the emergency situation.
I can't **make sense of** either the Chinese or Korean languages, and that's why I can't tell them apart.

7. **to take exception to**—to disagree with, to dislike

   Usual subjects: people
   Usual NPs: plan, idea, proposal; statement, remark

   The chairman tried to put the measure through the official committee without looking into it, but several committee members **took exception to** his plan.
   In his speech, the economist put unemployment above inflation as a cause of national concern, but other experts **took exception to** his statement.
   I don't like when my brother **takes exception to** my ideas, whether or not they are good.

8. **to find fault with**—to criticize, to speak badly about

   Usual subjects: people
   Usual NPs: people; people's actions; situation, plan

   The manager **found fault with** one worker for not putting forth any effort on the job.
   It's reasonable to **find fault with** anyone who tries to lead you on.
   He took exception to my plan because he **found fault with** it.

9. **to make light of**—to consider unimportant, to minimize the importance of

   Usual subjects: people
   Usual NPs: a situation, problem, mistake; pain, discomfort
   This idiom is used when someone doesn't think that something is important, but it really is.

   Although Joe never got over his emotional problem, now he tries to **make light of** it.
   Tom **made light of** his mistake, but his supervisor didn't at all.
   The injured football player wanted to continue playing so he **made light of** his serious pain.

10. **to take charge of**—to assume control of, to become responsible for

Usual subjects: people
Usual NPs: situation, matter; project, business, company

When the fire started, the police and firemen quickly **took charge of** the situation.

The secretary **took charge of** the matter until her boss returned.

The new president **took charge of** the company last spring when the old president resigned.

Class discussion:

Now that you have learned the meanings of the idioms and how to use them in sentences, go back to **Exercise I** and **Exercise II** and check your answers. As you do this, consider the following questions:

1. How many idioms did you guess correctly in **Exercise I?**

2. How much better did you do in **Exercise II?**

3. Are there any idiom meanings which are still not clear to you?

4. Is there anything you have noticed about the grammatical usage of these idioms?

IV. LEARNING THE GRAMMAR RULES

Part A   All of the idioms in this chapter, like the idioms in **Chapter 7,** are composed of a *transitive verb + preposition.* Again, the transitive verb will be followed by an object, and a noun phrase will follow the preposition.

Example:

transitive verb + preposition: **to keep an eye on**

The babysitter kept an eye on the child.

| subject | object | noun phrase |

verbal idiom

1. Is the preposition connected to the verb in the same way as in the previous chapter?

_____ Yes   _____ No

2. How do the idioms in this chapter differ from the idioms in **Chapter 7?**

Part B Look carefully at the following set of sentences. Some sentences are correct and some are incorrect (*). Answer the questions by comparing the sentences.

1. I carefully kept an eye on the child.
2. I kept a careful eye on the child.
3. *I carefully kept eyes on the child.
4. Tom unfairly took advantage of his friend.
5. Tom took unfair advantage of his friend.
6. *Tom took unfair disadvantage of his friend.

a. What is the difference between sentences #1 and #2?

b. Which other sentences can be compared in the same way?

c. What do sentences #3 and #6 tell you about the objects in these idioms?

d. Do you think that an adverb can be put anywhere inside the verbal idiom? Why or why not?

Each idiom in this chapter can only occur with one special object. The noun form in the object cannot change in any way. Very often an adjective form can be placed in front of the noun.

I *carefully* kept an eye on the child.   (adverb form)
I kept a *careful* eye on the child.   (adjective form)
*I kept careful *eyes* on the child.   (no change is possible)

As before, adverbs should not be placed anywhere inside the verbal idiom because an object is used.

Tom *unfairly* took advantage of his friend.   (correct position)
Tom took advantage of his friend *unfairly*.   (correct position)
*Tom took *unfairly* advantage of his friend.   (incorrect position)
†Tom took advantage *unfairly* of his friend.   (unusual position)

V. MULTIPLE-CHOICE EXERCISE

Choose the idiom from this chapter, or a previous one, which has the best meaning in the context below. No idiom is used twice as a correct answer. Be very careful about the grammar rules which you have learned.

1. The salesman _____ the customer _____ _____ a long discussion.

   a. drew . . . from
   b. left . . . to
   c. engaged . . . in

2. When my parents took two weeks off for a boat cruise, I _____ them _____ at the harbor.

   a. saw . . . off
   b. looked . . . up
   c. brought . . . up

3. If the problem is serious, _____ it; don't ignore it.

   a. put above
   b. take a stand on
   c. take advantage of

4. Do you think that you'll ever _____ a better position?

   a. keep up with
   b. work up to
   c. lose track of

5. The bill for our expensive dinner _____ $200.

   a. turned to
   b. came to
   c. took charge of

6. I look forward to meeting the famous professor because I have _____ him for many years.

   a. gone in for
   b. looked up to
   c. made light of

7. His advice was so helpful that I _____ thanking him the next time I saw him.

   a. made a point of
   b. devoted to
   c. took advantage of

8. How did such a bad mistake _____?

   a. bring about
   b. come about
   c. fall through

9. He's so slow at understanding difficult ideas that I doubt he'll ever _____.

   a. give up
   b. catch on
   c. come up with

10. You shouldn't _____ a serious problem; deal with it as though it were very important.

   a. find fault with
   b. make light of
   c. keep an eye on

VI. WRITING EXERCISE

Please answer each question by using the idiom in a meaningful, grammatical sentence.

1. Have you ever taken unfair advantage of your parents?

2. Have you lost track of any friends from your hometown?

3. What does a driver have to keep an eye on?

4. Do you take a stand on political matters? Why or why not?

5. If you hurt someone, what should you make a point of doing?

6. Why do foreign students sometimes find it difficult to make sense of TV programs in English?

7. Why would you take exception to someone's bad plan?

8. When is it necessary for a manager to find fault with his workers?

9. Why would a person try to make light of an important problem?

10. Who takes charge of a company when the president takes off a couple of weeks for vacation?

9

Transitive Verbs with Prepositions (Type III)

to have on one's mind
to bring into focus
to take at one's word
to get off one's chest
to bring into the open

to lay to rest
to pull to pieces
to put to use
to take into account
to play by ear

I. GUESSING THE MEANING FROM CONTEXT

Guess the meaning of each idiom as it is used in the following sentences. Provide either a one-word synonym or a definition. Underline the context clues as you are trying to guess the meaning.

1. I was very concerned about my problems; I **had** them **on my mind** all the time.

2. We touched on too many topics, so the group leader **brought** all of them **into focus** by summarizing our discussion.

3. You shouldn't doubt him when he claims that he's telling the truth; **take** him **at his word.**

4. I tried to hold back my real dislike for him, but I finally had to **get** my true feelings **off my chest.**

5. At first, the criminal left out part of his crime in his confession, but eventually he **brought** the whole thing **into the open.**

6. After the criminal told all the details of his crime, the police were able to **lay** the crime **to rest** and file it away.

7. The lawyer destroyed every argument of the opposing lawyer; he really **pulled** his arguments **to pieces!**

8. Don't go through your tax refund wastefully; **put** it **to use** _____
well.

9. Before the committee took a stand on the issue, it went into _____
the matter carefully by **taking** each member's opinion **into
account.**

10. The unpredictable situation might change at any moment, _____
so we'd better **play** it **by ear** as it develops, instead of deciding now.

Class discussion:

Decide which idioms were easy to guess and which were difficult.
Consider the importance of context clues in your decisions.

II. DEFINITION CORRESPONDENCE

Using **Exercise I** to help you, check your guesses by choosing
the correct idiom which corresponds to the definition you see on
the left side. Be sure to use context clues and to use the correct
grammar forms.

to have on one's mind   to lay to rest
to bring into focus   to pull to pieces
to take at one's word   to put to use
to get off one's chest   to take into account
to bring into the open   to play by ear

(to release one's
emotions)

1. His actions make me so upset that I have to _____

_____ my anger _____ .

(to consider)

2. I _____ many ideas _____ before

I choose the best way.

(to finally resolve)

3. My friend and I couldn't find an answer to our serious prob-

lem, but eventually we were able to _____ the

problem _____ with the helpful advice of a

counselor.

(to improvise)

4. I wish we could decide on a plan now, but it would be

smarter to _____ it _____ as the

situation changes.

(to make very clear)   5. At first they were confused about the project, but the consul-

tant _____ it _____ quite easily.

(to utilize well)   6. When you get a job after college, you're expected to _____

_____ your knowledge _____ in your

new duties.

(to reveal)   7. Although he didn't want to part with his secret, the police

made him _____ it _____ .

(to criticize very badly)   8. The manager _____ the worker _____

_____ for his very careless work.

(to worry about)   9. I can't sleep well at night because I _____ too

many problems _____ .

(to believe)   10. The witness insisted that he was telling the truth, so the

judge had no choice but to _____ him

_____ .

III. EXPLANATION OF THE IDIOMS

1. **to have on one's mind**—to worry about, to think constantly about

   Usual subjects: people
   Usual objects: problem, difficulty; many things, a lot, a great deal; a situation

   Don't bother me because I **have** a serious problem **on my mind.**
   The President engages himself in so many national matters; he **has** a great deal **on his mind.**
   The mother **had** her daughter's wedding **on her mind** all week.

2. **to bring into focus**—to make very clear; to summarize

   Usual subjects: people
   Usual objects: matter, issue, situation; problem

That lawyer can always come up with a good summary of the case which **brings** the issues **into focus.**

The new government of that country is too disorganized to **bring** its problems **into focus** and solve them.

3. **to take at one's word**—to believe that someone is telling the truth, to trust what someone says

   Usual subjects: people
   Usual objects: people

   I don't **take** him **at his word** because I think he's leading us on.

   They didn't make light of his promise to do it because they **take** him **at his word.**

   If you say that I can leave all my work to you while I'm gone, I'll **take** you **at your word!**

4. **to get off one's chest**—to finally release one's true feelings or emotions

   Usual subjects: people
   Usual objects: feelings; *it*

   After Tom got too angry, he **got** his feelings **off his chest.**

   When you get very upset, it's good to **get** it **off your chest.**

   She tried to hold her sadness back, but suddenly she **got** it **off her chest;** you should have seen how many tissues she used!

5. **to bring into the open**—to divulge, to reveal, to expose (a secret)

   Usual subjects: people; investigation, court trial; newspaper
   Usual objects: feeling, attitude, truth; question, matter; crime; mistake

   The husband **brought** his feelings about their marriage **into the open.**

   The police investigation **brought** the crime **into the open.**

   The newspaper article **brought** the political scandal **into the open.**

6. **to lay to rest**—to resolve, to finally end, to remove doubt about

   Usual subjects: people; explanation, statement
   Usual objects: matter, problem, issue; story, rumor; doubt, uncertainty

   After the committee members found out the best solution, they were able to **lay** their problem **to rest.**

The actress **laid** the rumor about her drug habit **to rest** by bringing the truth into the open: she had cancer.

The politician's explanation **laid** any doubt **to rest** about his financial deals; he was completely innocent.

7. **to pull to pieces**—to criticize very badly, to find serious fault with

Usual subjects: people
Usual objects: people; suggestions, idea, theory; argument, evidence

Politicians always try to **pull** their opponent's ideas **to pieces.**

The famous scientist **pulled** the new theory **to pieces** because it was very unscientific.

The defense lawyer **pulled** the prosecution's evidence **to pieces,** so the defendant was found not guilty by the judge.

8. **to put to** (good) **use**—to make effective use of, to utilize well

Usual subjects: people
Usual objects: money, savings; time; labor, work, effort
This idiom usually has the adjective "good" preceding the noun phrase.

Smart businessmen **put** their money **to use** in the best investments.

If you want to draw value from your education, **put** your study time **to good use.**

Everyone pitched in and **put** their efforts **to good use,** so soon we had accomplished our purpose.

9. **to take into account**—to consider (as part of), to include in consideration

Usual subjects: people
Usual objects: matter, problem, situation; details, circumstances, factors
This idiom is used when something should be considered in a larger context.

The judge **took** the man's poor financial situation **into account** when he made a court decision: the man paid for only half the damages.

I know I was wrong to do that, but please **take** the special circumstances **into account** before you decide on the punishment.

In world economics, financial experts must **take** many factors **into account** when they advise world leaders.

10. **to play by ear**—to improvise, to make plans as something occurs or develops

Usual subjects: people
Usual objects: matter, situation; *it*
The pronoun form *it* is most often used in this idiom.

The world leaders decided to **play** it **by ear** as they kept up constant telephone communication about new developments in the international crisis.
It's impossible to put forth a firm plan in advance because there are too many variables; we'll have to **play** it **by ear.**

Class discussion:

Now that you have learned the meanings of the idioms and how to use them in sentences, go back to **Exercise I** and **Exercise II** and check your answers. As you do this, consider the following questions:

1. How many idioms did you guess correctly in **Exercise I?**

2. How much better did you do in **Exercise II?**

3. Are there any idiom meanings which are still not clear to you?

4. Is there anything you have noticed about the grammatical usage of these idioms?

IV. LEARNING THE GRAMMAR RULES

Part A   All of the idioms in this chapter, like those in **Chapters 7** and **8,** are composed of a *transitive verb + preposition.* It is again true that the verb will be followed by an object, and a noun phrase will follow the preposition.

Example:

transitive verb + preposition: **to take into account**

The instructor	took	my illness	into account.
subject	verb	object	prep. phrase

verbal idiom

1. How is the preposition connected to the verb? To the noun phrase?

2. How do the idioms in this chapter differ from the idioms in **Chapter 8?**

Part B Look carefully at the following set of sentences. Some sentences are correct and some are incorrect (*). Answer the questions by comparing the sentences.

1. Mary put her scholarship to good use.
2. *The criminal brought into the truth the open.
3. *Mary put her scholarship to good uses.
4. The criminal brought the truth into the open.

a. What is the difference between sentences #1 and #3?

b. What does this tell you about the noun following the preposition in each of these idioms?

c. What is the difference between sentences #2 and #4?

d. Fill in the appropriate answers:

A _____ will never precede the _____

of a sentence.

Each idiom in this chapter can only occur with one special noun in the noun phrase following the preposition. The noun cannot change form in any way.

Mary put her scholarship to *use.*   (correct form)
Mary put her scholarship to *good use.*   (correct form with
                                                            adjective added)
*Mary put her scholarship to good *uses.*(no change in form
                                                            is possible)

As before, adverbs should *not* be placed anywhere inside the verbal idiom because an object is used.

V. MULTIPLE-CHOICE EXERCISE

Choose the idiom from this chapter, or a previous one, which has the best meaning in the context below. No idiom is used twice as a correct answer. Be very careful about the grammar rules which you have learned.

1. I made so many mistakes that I had to _____ my work _____.

   a. do . . . over
   b. put . . . to good use
   c. play . . . by ear

2. Your support for me would _____ truth _____ my claim in court.

   a. put . . . above
   b. bring . . . up
   c. lend . . . to

3. The counsel of the defendant looks so serious and concerned that he must _____ something _____.

   a. devote . . . to
   b. have . . . on his mind
   c. take . . . into account

4. Why did you refuse to help him when he _____ _____ you?

   a. turned to
   b. talked over
   c. made a point of

5. I'm so tired and tied down in my work that I can't _____ my work life and my home life _____.

   a. tell . . . apart
   b. put . . . above
   c. lay . . . to rest

6. Some people like to give away secrets while others don't like to _____ them _____.

   a. pull . . . to pieces
   b. lay . . . to rest
   c. bring . . . into the open

7. I'll never get an A in this class if I can't _____ the other students.

   a. hang on to
   b. keep up with
   c. believe in

8. He carried out his tasks very well; I think everyone should _____ him for his fine effort.

   a. go in for
   b. get through to
   c. look up to

9. We don't have time to go into it today so let's _____ it _____ until next Monday.

   a. lay . . . to rest
   b. put . . . off
   c. have . . . on our minds

10. After the debater found fault with his opponent, his opponent completely _____ the debater's criticisms _____ and won the debate easily.

    a. did . . . over
    b. pointed . . . out
    c. pulled . . . to pieces

VI. WRITING EXERCISE

Please answer each question by using the idiom in a meaningful, grammatical sentence.

1. What do students usually have on their minds?

2. How does an instructor bring an idea into focus?

3. Should you always take someone at his word? Why or why not?

4. When would a person have to get something off his chest?

5. Why don't some people bring their mistakes into the open?

6. How do you lay your problems to rest?

7. Why do politicians try to pull other politicians to pieces?

8. How are you putting your savings to use?

9. To decide on a divorce case, what does a judge have to take into account about the couple?

10. In general, is it better to plan things carefully or to play them by ear? Why?

10

Transitive Verbs with Particles and Prepositions

to bring around to   to fill in on
to let in on   to get out of
to turn over to   to take up with
to set aside for   to leave up to
to talk over with   to have (it) out with

I. GUESSING THE MEANING FROM CONTEXT

Guess the meaning of each idiom as it is used in the following sentences. Provide either a one-word synonym or a definition. Underline the context clues as you are trying to guess the meaning.

1. At first he stuck to his own opinion stubbornly, but finally we **brought** him **around to** our way of thinking. _____

2. For a long time my friend didn't want to bring his problem into the open, but eventually he **let** me **in on** it so I could help him. _____

3. Because old Mr. Jones would never get over his serious illness, he couldn't manage his business, so he **turned** it **over to** his son. _____

4. I know that I need a lot of money if I want to take off one year from work in order to travel, so each month I am **setting** $100 **aside for** this purpose. _____

5. He wanted to go into the matter more deeply so he asked to **talk** it **over with** me next week. _____

6. Since the manager knew nothing about the proposed project, his secretary **filled** him **in on** the important facts. _____

7. The professor only touched very briefly on various uninteresting ideas, so Joe couldn't **get** much **out of** the lecture. _____

8. I have no authority to approve your plan; you'll have to **take** it **up with** the president before you proceed.

    _____

9. If you really don't care where your family settles down, then **leave** it **up to** your wife to find the best place.

    _____

10. Because Alice couldn't hold back her deep anger any more, she decided to open up and **have** it **out with** her selfish boyfriend.

    _____

Class discussion:

Decide which idioms were easy to guess and which were difficult. Consider the importance of context clues in your decisions.

II. DEFINITION CORRESPONDENCE

Using **Exercise I** to help you, check your guesses by choosing the correct idiom which corresponds to the definition you see on the left side. Be sure to use context clues and to use the correct grammar forms.

to bring around to	to fill in on
to let in on	to get out of
to turn over to	to take up with
to set aside for	to leave up to
to talk over with	to have (it) out with

(to save for)   1. In order to buy her a nice Christmas present, Jeff _____

_____ money _____ a beautiful gift.

(to discuss with)   2. If you'd like to open up about your problems, why don't you

_____ them _____ a counselor?

(to gain from)   3. The lecture was so boring that I didn't _____

anything _____ it at all.

(to give the decision to)   4. Since the manager wouldn't take a stand on the important

issue, he _____ it _____ the com-

pany president.

(to inform about)   5. The advisor _____ the politician _____

_____ the details of his speech because the politician had no time to brush up on the speech himself.

(to discuss angrily with)   6. For a long time my resentment of him grew until finally I had to _____ it _____ him.

(to give control to)   7. Because of the violent revolution, the military government had to_____ the government_____ the people who had won.

(to change someone's mind about)   8. At first we couldn't clear up his misunderstanding about our opinion, but eventually we were able to _____ him _____ our point of view.

(to allow to know)   9. I shouldn't have _____ him _____ _____ my serious situation because soon everyone knew.

(to consult with)   10. When the teenager wanted his own apartment, he _____ _____ the idea _____ his parents.

III. EXPLANATION OF THE IDIOMS

1. **to bring around to**—to change someone's mind about, to convince about

   Usual subjects: people
   Usual objects: people
   Usual NPs: point of view, way of thinking, opinion, side (of an argument)

   In a strike situation, workers try to **bring** management **around to** their point of view by refusing to work.
   Why did it take so long to **bring** him **around to** your opinion?
   At first I was arguing against him, but then he **brought** me **around to** his side.

2. **to let in on**—to allow to know (a secret); to allow to take part in (a secret situation)

Usual subjects: people
Usual objects: people
Usual NPs: secret, scheme; secret plan or situation

He **let** her **in on** his secret so that they could talk it over and finally lay it to rest.
Since I needed more money for my new business plan, I **let** more investors **in on** it; they promised not to part with the private information.

3. **to turn over to**—1) to give control to, to give ownership to
2) to give to the police, to turn in (to the police)

#1 Usual subjects: *people* (owner, president, stockholders)
Usual objects: company, business; control, management
Usual NPs: *people* (new president, owner, buyer; associate, partner; brother, son)

Since the original owner was now too old to hold on to his business, he **turned** it **over to** a new buyer.
When the company president resigned to try for a better job, he **turned** control **over to** his associate.
Many times an owner will keep the business in the family by **turning** it **over to** a brother or son.

#2 Usual subjects: people
Usual objects: criminal, prisoner, convict; stolen property
Usual NPs: police, authorities

The storeowner **turned** the shoplifter **over to** the police.
Since I took exception to my neighbor's criminal activities, I **turned** him **over to** federal authorities.

4. **to set aside for**—to save for, to reserve for (a special purpose)

Usual subjects: people
Usual objects: money, a few dollars; time, *a period of time* (minute, hour, day, weekend)
Usual NPs: a special thing or activity

Will you be able to **set** some money **aside for** a nice vacation next summer?
The poor man made a point of **setting** a few dollars **aside for** an anniversary present for his wife.
Can you **set** an hour **aside for** a quiet dinner with me?
The busy executive **set** a weekend **aside for** a small trip with his family.

5. **to talk over with**—to discuss with

    Usual subjects: people
    Usual objects: matter, problem, plan; things
    Usual NPs: people

    I'd like to **talk** things **over with** you because I simply can't put up with it any longer.
    His wife **talked** things **over with** him for two hours in an effort to get through to him about their marital difficulties.

6. **to fill in on**—to inform about, to give current information about

    Usual subjects: people
    Usual objects: people
    Usual NPs: details, plan, project, latest development; any unknown situation

    The assistant **filled** his boss **in on** the details of the conference.
    The President had his advisor **fill** him **in on** the latest development in the national crisis.
    When he returned, the secretary **filled** the executive **in on** the week's activities.

7. **to get out of**—to gain from, to obtain from

    Usual subjects: people
    Usual objects: nothing, something, a lot, much; many ideas, much information; money, profit
    Usual NPs: speech, lecture, talk, discussion; class, course; book; business deal, arrangement, venture

    Unfortunately, I **got** nothing **out of** his poor lecture.
    I have **gotten** much useful information **out of** this business course, so I should **get** much money **out of** my first business venture.

8. **to take up with**—to consult with, to raise a subject with (usually a person of higher authority)

    Usual subjects: *people* (assistant, advisor, employee, secretary, student)
    Usual objects: matter, problem, issue, question
    Usual NPs: *people* (supervisor, manager, president, employer, boss, teacher)

    The assistant couldn't make a decision without authorization, so he **took** the matter **up with** his supervisor.
    The employee **took** the question of a raise **up with** his employer.
    Did the student **take** the grading issue **up with** his teacher?

9. **to leave up to**—to give the choice or decision to; to leave to

Usual subjects: people
Usual objects: choice, decision; matter, issue, *it*
Usual NPs: people

I **left** the choice of colors for the house **up to** my wife.
Since you don't want to decide, **leave** the matter **up to** your
boss when she returns.
He said that I could **leave** it **up to** him to carry out the job,
so I took him at his word.

10. **to have** (it) **out with**—to discuss angrily with (until something is laid to rest)

Usual subjects: people
Usual objects: *it*
Usual NPs: people

She couldn't live with her roommate's bad habits, so she **had**
it **out with** her; she promised to turn into a better roommate.
Should you **have** it **out with** a friend who constantly takes
unfair advantage of you?

Class discussion:

Now that you have learned the meanings of the idioms and how
to use them in sentences, go back to **Exercise I** and **Exercise II**
and check your answers. As you do this, consider the following
questions:

1. How many idioms did you guess correctly in **Exercise I?**

2. How much better did you do in **Exercise II?**

3. Are there any idiom meanings which are still not clear to you?

4. Is there anything you have noticed about the grammatical
usage of these idioms?

IV. LEARNING THE GRAMMAR RULES

Part A All of the idioms in this chapter are composed of a *transitive verb + particle + preposition*. An object will follow the verb
and a noun phrase will follow the preposition.

Example:

> transitive verb + particle + preposition: **to get out of**

The participants got many ideas out of the conference.
- subject
- verbal idiom (got ... out of)
- object (many ideas)
- noun phrase (the conference)

1. How is the particle connected to the verb?

2. How is the preposition connected to the verb? To the noun phrase?

3. Where could a manner adverb be placed? Where would it be wrong to place an adverb?

Part B Look carefully at the following set of sentences. Some sentences are correct and some are incorrect (*). Answer the questions by comparing the sentences.

1. You should set aside time for a meeting.
2. You should set time aside for a meeting.
3. I got many ideas out of the conference.
4. *I got out many ideas of the conference.
5. I turned it over to my associates.
6. *I turned over it to my associates.

a. What is the difference between sentences #1 and #2?

b. Why is sentence #4 incorrect and which sentence is the correct form?

c. Fill in the proper answers:

The normal position for an _____ is before the

particle, but in some idioms it may be placed after the

_____ .

d. What do sentences #5 and #6 tell you about pronoun objects?

Although the normal position for the object is before the particle, with certain idioms the object may follow the particle.

I got *many ideas* out of the conference.   (correct position)
I took *the matter* up with Joe.   (correct position)
*I got out *many ideas* of the conference.   (incorrect position)
I took up *the matter* with Joe.   (correct position)

Generally, the particle is movable if the idiom is correct even when the preposition and noun phrase (NP) are removed. If the preposition and noun phrase cannot be removed, then the particle can never be placed before the object.

I took the matter *up* with Joe.	(normal position)
We took the matter *up*.	(prep. and NP removed)
I took *up* the matter with Joe.	(particle can move)
We took *up* the matter.	(prep. and NP removed)

I got many ideas *out* of the conference.	(normal position)
*I got many ideas *out*.	(prep. and NP can't be removed)
*I got *out* many ideas of the conference.	(particle can't move)
*I got *out* many ideas.	(prep. and NP can't be removed)

A pronoun form will always be placed before the particle.

I turned *it* over to my assistant.   (correct position)
*I turned over *it* to my assistant.   (incorrect position)

V. MULTIPLE-CHOICE EXERCISE

Choose the idiom from this chapter, or a previous one, which has the best meaning in the context below. No idiom is used twice as a correct answer. Be very careful about the grammar rules which you have learned.

1. The class was so good that I _____ a lot _____ it.

   a. put . . . above
   b. got . . . out of
   c. put . . . to use

2. No one could _____ him _____ the terrible period after his wife's death; he went insane.

   a. pull . . . through
   b. let . . . in on
   c. put . . . through

3. Why is it hard for me to _____ this difficult book?

   a. make sense of
   b. lose track of
   c. keep up

4. The problem _____ because a worker was careless.

   a. brought about
   b. looked into
   c. came about

5. I want to get the problem off my chest so I'll _____ _____ it _____ him.

    a. have . . . out with
    b. engage . . . in
    c. leave . . . up to

6. He's ignorant of our plans; let's _____ him _____ them.

    a. turn . . . over to
    b. leave . . . to
    c. fill . . . in on

7. The student _____ a good question, which the teacher was able to answer.

    a. brought up
    b. held over
    c. took up

8. At first he _____ me _____ about the secret, but finally he let me in on the truth.

    a. brought . . . into the open
    b. brought . . . into focus
    c. led . . . on

9. He didn't care at all that he hurt my feelings; I _____ that fact _____ him.

    a. confuse . . . with
    b. hold . . . against
    c. draw . . . from

10. The engine needed repair because it was _____ too much smoke.

    a. giving off
    b. drawing from
    c. giving away

VI. WRITING EXERCISE

Please answer each question by using each idiom in a meaningful, grammatical sentence.

1. How would you bring someone around to your point of view?

2. Should a husband let his wife in on his secrets? Why or why not?

3. If a teacher were sick, who would he turn his class over to?

4. What are you setting aside money for?

5. Who do you talk your problems over with?

6. What does a secretary fill her boss in on?

7. What can you get out of a movie?

8. What might you take up with your parents?

9. Who should you leave medical decisions up to?

10. If you're upset with someone, do you have it out with him or her? Why or why not?

11

Review of Transitive Verbal Idioms

I. COMPARISON OF TRANSITIVE FORMS

In **Chapter 4** you learned that intransitive verbs can combine with different particles and/or prepositions to form verbal idioms. This fact is also true of transitive verbs, and there are several idioms which can change form, and in some cases, meaning, in the same basic ways.

A   One change occurs when a *preposition* is added to certain *transitive verb + particle* idioms. You have seen three examples of this. The transitive verbal idiom **to fill in,** meaning "to inform," can join with the preposition *on* to form **to fill in on,** meaning "to inform about."

The person who saw the crime **filled** the police **in.**
The person **filled** the police **in on** the crime.

Also, the idiom **to talk over,** meaning "to discuss," can join with the preposition *with* to form **to talk over with,** meaning "to discuss with."

My wife and I **talked** our problem **over.**
I **talked** our problem **over with** my wife.

The same situation applies in the case of **to take up,** meaning "to begin work on," and **to take up with,** meaning "to consult with." However, notice that in this case a change in meaning exists.

When he finished one job, he **took up** the next one.
I **took up** the problem **with** my supervisor.

Many verb + particle idioms cannot join with a preposition in this way, so you must learn which idioms can. You also have to be very careful about the position of objects and any major changes in meaning. One other idiom can commonly join with prepositions.

to try out—to test, to check the function of
to try out on—to test something by using someone

The company president **tried out** the new product.
The company **tried** the new product **out on** some supermarket customers.

B.   You probably expect that some of the *transitive verb + particle + preposition* idioms in **Chapter 10** were made by adding a preposition to a transitive verb + particle idiom. The idioms **fill in on, take up with,** and **talk over with** were examples. There are four other verbal idioms you have studied which can be used both with and without a preposition. When a preposition is used, a noun phrase will follow.

1. **to bring around to**—to change someone's mind about
    to bring around—to change someone's mind

    We **brought** him **around to** our way of thinking.
    After explaining our way of thinking, we **brought** him **around.**

2. **to set aside for**—to save for, to reserve for
    to set aside—to save, to reserve

    I **set aside** $20 **for** a birthday gift.
    To get a nice gift, I **set aside** $20.

3. **to turn over to**—to give control to
    to turn over—to give control

    He **turned** the company **over to** the larger corporation.
    He **turned over** his company when the large corporation bought it.

4. **to have it out with**—to finally argue with
    to have it out—to finally argue

    For a long time I wanted to **have it out with** Joe.
    When Joe and I finally met, we **had it out.**

In all of these cases, the addition of a preposition causes no significant change in meaning. However, this is not always the case, so you have to pay careful attention to possible variations, and do your best to learn each special situation.

II. OTHER GRAMMATICAL FORMS OF TRANSITIVE VERBAL IDIOMS

As was true for intransitive idioms, it is important for you to know how to transform transitive idioms into other grammatical forms in order to be able to use them in different situations.

A. Nominalized Forms

Many transitive verbal idioms can be used in a nominalized form. Most forms combine without using a hyphen (−), but some do, so you again have to memorize the different cases as you learn them. Compare the following:

We **tried out** the new machine.
We gave the machine **a tryout.**

She **made up** her face.
She put on **makeup.**

The company **gave away** many gifts.
The company had a gift **giveaway.**

The military **took over** the country.
The country suffered a military **takeover.**

How many students **make up** this class?
What is the **makeup** of this class?
What is the **make-up** of this class?

You can see that nominalized forms are most useful with transitive verb + particle combinations. There are many more verbal idioms which transform into noun forms in this way, and knowing how and when to use the noun forms correctly can increase your ability to communicate effectively.

B. Passive Forms

Sometimes the subject of a verbal idiom is not very important, and we want to stress the object of the sentence. Objects used with transitive verbal idioms can move to subject position after the unimportant subject has either been moved to the end of the sentence or removed completely.

Transitive verb + particle forms

We **tried** the machine **out** carefully.
The machine **was tried out** carefully.   (movable particle forms)
We **tried out** the machine carefully.

You should **do** your work **over** soon.   (immovable particle form—
Your work should **be done over** soon.   Type A)

The job **tied down** the worker.   (immovable particle form—
The worker **was tied down** (by his job.)   Type B)

Transitive verb + preposition forms

His friends **held** the crime **against** Joe.   (Type I)
The crime **was held against** Joe (by his friends)

I **took** full **advantage of** my new car.   (Type II)
Full **advantage was taken of** my new car.

The police **kept an eye on** the criminal.   (also Type II)
An eye was kept on the criminal.

The teacher **brought** the idea **into focus.**   (Type III)
The idea **was brought into focus** (by the teacher).

Transitive verb + particle + preposition forms

We **brought** Joe **around to** our way of thinking.
Joe **was brought around to** our way of thinking.

As was true with intransitive verbal forms, some transitive verbal idioms can more easily be made passive than others; at times a passive form sounds very awkward, as in the following examples:

I **lost track of** my pen.
*****Track was lost of** my pen.   (incorrect form)

Bob **had** many problems **on his mind.**
*****Many problems **were had on Bob's mind.**   (incorrect form)

III. PARAGRAPH COMPOSITION

Please write a short paragraph using each group of idioms listed below. Organize your thoughts before you start to write so that the paragraph is logical and well-formed. A situation is suggested for your use.

A. A company is having an informal meeting about advertising techniques.

    (to kick around, to give away, to try out, to find out)

_____

_____

_____

_____

_____

_____

_____

B. Two people had an argument about a lie one of them told the other.

   (to lead on, to find fault with, to get off one's chest, to lay to rest)

_____

_____

_____

_____

_____

_____

_____

C. A person is explaining about his busy life and why he can't take a vacation.

   (to be engaged in, to have on one's mind, to tie down, to take off)

_____

_____

_____

_____

_____

_____

_____

D. A student was discussing the problems between his active social life and difficult academic life.

   (to run around with, to keep up with, to put above, to devote to)

_____

_____

_____

_____

_____

_____

_____

IV. ADDITIONAL CLASS ACTIVITIES

A. Role-Play Topics

The class should divide into small groups, and each group should create a dialogue which incorporates the suggested topic(s) and appropriate idioms. If possible, the groups should take turns presenting their dialogues to the rest of the class, afterwards discussing the differences in the presentations.

1. A business executive has been on vacation. When he returns to work, he will have a meeting with his secretary about an important decision which was made in his absence. What do they talk about?

   Suggested idioms: take up, fill in on, leave up to, take into account

2. A student's parents are concerned that their son, whose education they are paying for, is wasting time with his friends and is not succeeding in school, so they have a serious discussion with him. What do they say to each other?

   Suggested idioms: put through, lose track of, carry out, put forth

3. Your friend is having some personal problems and you would like to help him, but he is reluctant to talk about them. You

try to convince him to discuss them with you. What do you say, and how does he respond?

Suggested idioms: have on one's mind, pull through, let in on, bring into the open

B. Discussion Topics

1. Again, evaluate your feelings while you were presenting your dialogues. Did you feel comfortable using the idioms in your presentation? Did they help you to express your ideas better?

2. Do any of the new idioms you learned in Section II have equivalent forms in your own language? Which ones? What are the similarities or differences?

3. Try to take advantage of opportunities to talk with English speakers, if possible, and note some idiomatic expressions which you hear. Bring in a few examples to class for discussion.

NOMINAL, ADJECTIVAL, AND ADVERBIAL IDIOMS

12

Nominal Forms: Pairs of Nouns

flesh and blood   odds and ends
heart and soul   rank and file
part and parcel   ups and downs
wear and tear   give and take
pins and needles   ins and outs

I. GUESSING THE MEANING FROM CONTEXT

Guess the meaning of each idiom as it is used in the following sentences. Provide either a synonym or a definition. Underline the context clues which help you to guess the meaning.

1. All three of his children look just like him because they are his own **flesh and blood.** _____

2. The volunteer was so dedicated to the politician that he put his **heart and soul** into all his work. _____

3. Tom's quick temper is **part and parcel** of his personality; he was born with it and will never change. _____

4. After 100,000 miles, my car has suffered a lot of **wear and tear,** especially on the old engine. _____

5. The movie was so scary that the audience was constantly on **pins and needles;** they were sitting on the edges of their seats. _____

6. Before going on vacation, Joe had quite a few **odds and ends** to take care of, like loan payments and various errands. _____

7. Although the supervisors and managers received salary increases, the **rank and file** didn't. _____

8. Marriages cannot always be perfect; every couple should expect some **ups and downs.** _____

9. If the couple believes in **give and take,** they can solve most of their disagreements. _____

10. That older politician is very successful because he knows the **in and outs** of government business well. _____

Class discussion:

Decide which idioms were easy to guess and which were difficult. Consider the importance of context clues in your decisions.

II. DEFINITION CORRESPONDENCE

Using **Exercise I** to help you, check your guesses by choosing the correct idiom which corresponds to the definition you see on the left side. Be sure to use context clues and to use the correct grammar forms.

flesh and blood   odds and ends
heart and soul   rank and file
part and parcel   ups and downs
wear and tear   give and take
pins and needles   ins and outs

(cooperation)   1. A successful relationship between business partners depends on _____ on decisions.

(family)   2. Of course Tom is a prominent lawyer like me; he's my own _____ , isn't he?

(basic part)   3. Facing danger and risking life are _____ of a policeman's job.

(damage)   4. Because they have seven active children, their furniture gets a lot of _____ .

(difficulties)   5. The unlucky actor could only get a few good movie roles; his life was full of _____ .

(all the details)   6. To be successful as a businessman, you have to know the _____ of the business world.

(excitement) 7. We were on _____ waiting to know whether we

would have a baby boy or girl.

(ordinary people) 8. Rich people get many tax deductions; it's the

_____ who suffer the most.

(full energy) 9. The student wanted so much to graduate that all of his

_____ went into his difficult studies.

(various items) 10. Before taking a lunch break, the secretary had some_____

_____ to finish up quickly for her boss.

III. EXPLANATION OF THE IDIOMS

1. **flesh and blood**—one's family or blood relatives; kin

   This idiom is preceded by a possessive pronoun, and often by the word *own*.

   In a disaster, people take care of their own **flesh and blood** before helping their neighbors.

   Of course I'm proud of my daughter; she's my own **flesh and blood.**

2. **heart and soul**—one's entire energy, all of one's efforts

   The idiom usually occurs with the verbal idiom **put into,** and is preceded by a possessive pronoun.

   If you put your **heart and soul** into your work, you'll succeed.

   The opera singer put her **heart and soul** into the difficult performance.

3. **part and parcel**—a basic part, an integral portion

   No article precedes this idiom; the verb *be* is usually used.

   Profit-making is **part and parcel** of all business activities.
   Why does poverty have to be **part and parcel** of life in undeveloped countries?
   Sally's selfishness is **part and parcel** of her real character.

4. **wear and tear**—damage, deterioration caused by frequent use

This idiom is often used in reference to machines; a quantity word usually precedes the idiom.

When I rented out my piano to a stranger, it suffered some **wear and tear.**

My car has received a lot of **wear and tear** from driving to work everyday.

Joggers always put much **wear and tear** on their running shoes.

5. **pins and needles**—a condition of great excitement or nervousness

This idiom is usually preceded by *on;* the verb *sit* is commonly used when the idiom means *nervousness.*

The scary lightning and thunder storm had me on **pins and needles** all evening; it was fun!

Waiting for the important job interview, Mary sat on **pins and needles.**

6. **odds and ends**—various items; different tasks

This idiom is not preceded by an article; the adjective *some* or *various* often precedes it.

John made a fast dinner by using some **odds and ends** from the night before.

The reporter discovered the political crime because he had gathered various **odds and ends** of secret government information.

I did some **odds and ends** around the house before I turned on the TV.

7. **rank and file**—common workers; ordinary people

This idiom is usually used with a definite article, and sometimes is used as a compound noun form.

The **rank and file** in the factory wanted higher wages.

The **rank and file** in the U.S. are generally uninvolved in world affairs.

The **rank-and-file** employees went on strike for shorter hours and longer vacations.

8. **ups and downs**—good and bad times; difficulties

This idiom includes both bad and good periods of life, but it is only used during bad times. A possessive pronoun often precedes it.

The business had its **ups and downs** before it really became successful.

All married couples have their **ups and downs,** but they usually survive.

9. **give and take**—cooperation, compromise, concession

This idiom means that two or more people must share in making decisions in which an exchange of ideas or compromise is involved. No article is used.

If married couples don't believe in **give and take,** then they will suffer ups and downs.
Give and take is part and parcel of living closely with several roommates.

10. **ins and outs**—all the details, the important parts

A definite article is used with this idiom.

The corporate president knows all the **ins and outs** of the business world, both good and bad.
Students must learn all of the **ins and outs** of succeeding in school in order to do well.

Class discussion:

Now that you have learned the meanings of the idioms and how to use them in sentences, go back to **Exercise I** and **Exercise II** and check your answers. As you do this, consider the following questions:

1. How many idioms did you guess correctly in **Exercise I?**

2. How much better did you do in **Exercise II?**

3. Are there any idiom meanings which are still not clear to you?

4. Is there anything you have noticed about the grammatical usage of these idioms?

IV. LEARNING THE GRAMMAR RULES

Part A The nominal idioms in this chapter are formed from different parts of grammar, such as verbs, prepositions, and real nouns. These idioms can be used as subjects, objects, or as noun phrases after prepositions.

Examples:

Ups and downs are a part of life.   (prepositions)
— subject —

The athlete put his heart and soul into it.   (nouns)
             — object —

Marriage is a matter of <u>give and take.</u>   (verbs)
                          noun phrase

1. What word is used to join the verbs, prepositions, and nouns?

2. What is the difference between the first idiom above and the other two idioms?

Part B Look at the following sets of sentences. Some sentences are correct and some are incorrect (*). Answer the questions by comparing the sentences.

Set 1

1. The manager put his heart and soul into his work.
2. *The manager put his heart or soul into his work.
3. *The car suffered a lot of tear and wear.
4. The car suffered a lot of wear and tear.

a. How does sentence #2 differ from #1?

b. How does sentence #3 differ from #4?

With these idioms, the pair of forms can only be joined by the conjunction *and.* In addition, the order of the forms is fixed. The two words *cannot* exchange position in any situation.

The manager put his *heart and soul*   (correct conjunction)
into his work.
*The manager put his *heart or soul* into   (incorrect conjunction)
it.
The car suffered a lot of *wear and tear.*   (correct order)
*The car suffered a lot of *tear and wear.*   (incorrect order)

Set 2

1. I accomplished many odds and ends.
2. *I accomplished an odd and end.
3. These people are my flesh and blood.
4. *These people are my fleshes and bloods.

a. What do sentences #1 and #2 tell you about plural nominal forms?

b. What do sentences #3 and #4 tell you about singular nominal forms?

It is also important to remember that the singular forms can never be made plural and, likewise, that the plural forms cannot be made singular.

I accomplished a lot of *odds and ends.*   (correct plural form)
*I accomplished an *odd and end.*   (incorrect singular form)
These people are my *flesh and blood.*   (correct singular form)
*These people are my *fleshes and bloods.*   (incorrect plural form)

Regardless of whether the idioms were formed from verbs, prepositions, or nouns, the pairs of forms joined by *and* are considered to be real *noun forms.* This fact, along with the fact that these forms have special meanings, is why we call them idioms.

V. MULTIPLE-CHOICE EXERCISE

Choose the idiom from this chapter which has the best meaning in the context below. No idiom is used twice as a correct answer. Be careful about the grammar rules which you have learned.

1. Tom won't buy that old car because it has too much _____ _____ on it.
   a. ups and downs
   b. odds and ends
   c. wear and tear

2. My _____ were very kind to me when I was seriously ill.
   a. heart and soul
   b. rank and file
   c. flesh and blood

3. The criminal knows the _____ of successful robberies.
   a. part and parcel
   b. ins and outs
   c. ups and downs

4. Reaching a difficult agreement is a matter of _____ .
   a. give and take
   b. odds and ends
   c. part and parcel

5. Alone in the house at night without electricity, I was on _____ .
   a. heart and soul
   b. ups and downs
   c. pins and needles

VI. WRITING EXERCISE

Please answer each question or statement by using each idiom in a meaningful, grammatical sentence.

1. Which of your flesh and blood do you love the most?

2. What work do you put your heart and soul into?

3. What bad actions are part and parcel of war?

4. How do people put wear and tear on their cars?

5. In what situation would you be on pins and needles?

6. What kinds of odds and ends do housewives do around the house?

7. Why are the rank and file important in any country?

8. How do psychiatrists help people who have bad ups and downs?

9. Suggest a reason why marriage is a matter of give and take.

10. Why is it important to know the ins and outs of your work or job?

13
Nominal Forms: Adjective + Noun Combinations

last straw   second thoughts
close call   old hand
hot air   eager beaver
big shot   lost cause
white lie   small talk

I. GUESSING THE MEANING FROM CONTEXT

Guess the meaning of each idiom as it is used in the following sentences. Provide either a synonym or a definition. Underline the context clues which help you to guess the meaning.

1. Joe has borrowed money three times without paying me back, and now he wants $50! That's the **last straw!**   _____

2. I had a **close call** when a big truck nearly hit me as I was crossing the street.   _____

3. He thinks and talks as if he knows everything, but he really doesn't; he's full of **hot air.**   _____

4. My friend thinks he's a **big shot** because he has some responsibilities in the city mayor's office.   _____

5. When I said I liked her dinner, which really was terrible, I told a **white lie** because I didn't want to hurt her feelings.   _____

6. At first Mary agreed to marry John, but soon she was having **second thoughts.**   _____

7. Because Mr. Smith knows the ins and outs of plumbing, he's an **old hand** at it.   _____

8. Joe puts his heart and soul into his work, so that everyone thinks he's a real **eager beaver.**   _____

9. I'm afraid that there's no way we can fix your old car; you'd   _____ better get rid of it because it's a **lost cause.**

10. At most parties, people socialize by engaging in a lot of in-   _____ formal **small talk.**

Class discussion:

Decide which idioms were easy to guess and which were not. Consider the importance of context clues in your decisions.

II. DEFINITION CORRESPONDENCE

Using **Exercise I** to help you, check your guesses by choosing the correct idiom which corresponds to the definition you see on the left side. Be sure to use context clues and to use the correct grammar forms.

last straw	second thoughts
close call	old hand
hot air	eager beaver
big shot	lost cause
white lie	small talk

(important person)
1. Some policemen think they are _____ because of the legal power they have.

(enthusiastic worker)
2. An employee may be considered an _____ if he works very hard in order to please his boss.

(final annoyance)
3. When the baby started crying again for the fourth time, that was the _____ .

(informal conversation)
4. Some women like to contact each other on the telephone for some _____ .

(kind untruth)
5. Because I really didn't like his new suit at all, I told him a little _____ .

(experienced worker)
6. Mike is an _____ at fixing cars; he has repaired hundreds of them with no complaints from his customers.

(narrow escape)   7. The two airplanes had a _____ when they al-

most hit each other in the sky over San Francisco.

(hopeless situation)   8. We tried to save the damaged boat from sinking in the sea,

but it was a _____ .

(reconsideration)   9. The criminal had _____ about robbing the

bank after he saw the new security guard.

(exaggerated talk)   10. Big shots often are people who think they are wise but who

really are full of _____ .

III. EXPLANATION OF THE IDIOMS

1. **last straw**—1) final annoyance which results in a loss of patience

          2) final trouble which results in defeat

   This idiom is always used with a definite article; it usually is preceded by *that was*.

   First Tom, Dick, and Mary refused to help me; when my best friend, Joe, also refused, that was the **last straw.**
   Last week my car's door broke, and yesterday the radio stopped working; when the engine failed today, that was the **last straw!**
   After losing three difficult soccer games, our team lost to a very easy team; that was the **last straw!**

2. **close call**—narrow escape (from danger), close shave; a situation where someone almost was hurt seriously

   This idiom may be used in the plural.

   The motorcyclist had a **close call** when he fell off his bike; fortunately, he only received several small cuts.
   A thief attacked Jim with a knife, but was scared off by a police siren; that was a **close call** for Jim!
   A soldier in war can expect to face many **close calls.**

3. **hot air**—exaggerated talk; unproven ideas

   This idiom is often preceded by *a lot of* or *full of*, plus the verb *be*. No article is used.

   No one likes a person who thinks very highly of his own opinions but is really full of **hot air.**

John's speech was just a lot of **hot air** because he didn't really know what he was talking about.

4. **big shot**—important person

This idiom is considered informal, even slang; it is often used when a person is really less important than he thinks he is.

The politician knew a lot of **big shots** in business who donated a great deal of money to his campaign.
The world is full of people who think that they are **big shots,** but few ever get into the history books.
The students who are active in government and sports on our campus think they are **big shots,** but I don't think so.

5. **white lie**—kind untruth, small lie

This idiom is often used when the truth would hurt someone's feelings.

I told a **white lie** when I told him that I liked his poor painting.
A little **white lie** can save your flesh and blood from embarrassment.

6. **second thoughts**—reconsideration; change of mind or opinion

The idiom is usually used as the object of the verb *have*. No article is used, and the singular form cannot be used.

Tom had **second thoughts** about joining the military after high school graduation.
The brave soldier had no **second thoughts** as he attacked the enemy.

7. **old hand**—experienced worker; very knowledgeable person

The preposition *at* usually follows the idiom; a plural form may be used.

In the Old West, cowboys were **old hands** at controlling cattle.
The veteran yachtsman was an **old hand** at sailing boats.

8. **eager beaver**—enthusiastic worker; industrious person

This idiom is often used when someone is trying to impress his boss or superiors.

Eager beavers are often resented by other workers in an office.

If you really want to get ahead, it's better to be an **eager beaver.**

9. **lost cause**—hopeless situation, a situation which is a complete failure

   This idiom usually requires the verb *be* and an indefinite article.

   I think that your hope for give and take with that stubborn man is a **lost cause;** he rarely changes his mind.
   If a marriage has too many ups and downs, it may be a **lost cause.**

10. **small talk**—informal conversation, idle chit-chat

    No article can be used with this idiom, but quantity words often are.

    Some people are bothered by **small talk** because it's usually so boring.
    A little **small talk** between strangers can sometimes lead to a long-lasting relationship.

Class discussion:

Now that you have learned the meanings of the idioms and how to use them in sentences, go back to **Exercise I** and **Exercise II** and check your answers. As you do this, consider the following questions:

1. How many idioms did you guess correctly in **Exercise I?**

2. How much better did you do in **Exercise II?**

3. Are there any idiom meanings which are still not clear to you?

4. Is there anything you have noticed about the grammatical usage of these idioms?

IV. LEARNING THE GRAMMAR RULES

Part A The nominal idioms in this chapter are composed of various *adjective + noun* combinations. These combinations can be used as subjects, objects, or as noun phrases after prepositions.

Examples:

White lies are never good.
_____
subject

That was a very close call!
_____
object

I'm tired of small talk.
_____
noun phrase

1. What is the difference between the first idiom above and the other two idioms?

2. Do you think that the idioms could change form?

Part B Look carefully at the following sets of sentences. Some sentences are correct and some are incorrect (*). Answer the questions by comparing the sentences.

Set 1

1. I had second thoughts about marriage.
2. *I had a second thought about marriage.
3. Joe's actually full of hot air.
4. *Joe's actually full of hot airs.

a. How does sentence #2 differ from #1?

b. How does sentence #4 differ from #3?

c. What can you conclude about the nouns in these sentences?

Because the noun phrases in this chapter are idioms, certain unexplainable rules are used, just as was the case with all previous idioms in this book. One rule is that some of the nouns must be used in the plural, while others must be singular, and still others may vary in form.

I had *second thoughts* about marriage.   (plural form)
*I had a *second thought* about marriage. (singular form incorrect)
Joe's actually full of *hot air*.   (singular form)
*Joe's actually full of *hot airs*.   (plural form incorrect)
I had a *close call*.   (both singular and plural
I've had many *close calls*.   forms are correct)

Set 2

1. The race-car driver had many close calls.
2. *The race-car driver had many closer calls.
3. He's really an eager beaver about work.
4. *He's really a beaver about work.

a. What is the difference between sentences #1 and #2?

b. What is the difference between sentences #3 and #4?

c. What do these sentences tell you about the adjectives in these idioms?

The adjectives in these idioms are restricted in form. In general, only one particular adjective can be used with any noun form to create a special idiom, and this form usually cannot be deleted or altered in any way.

The race-car driver had many *close calls.* (correct form)
*The race-car driver had many *closer calls.* (no alteration possible)
He's really an *eager beaver* about work. (correct form)
*He's really a *beaver* about work. (no deletion possible)

There are no easy ways for learning the special rules which are used; only hard work, practice, and memorization will reward you the most.

V. MULTIPLE-CHOICE EXERCISE

Choose the idiom from this chapter, or the previous one, which has the best meaning in the context below. No idiom is used twice as a correct answer. Be careful about the grammar rules which you have learned.

1. The sixth time he called me at midnight was the _____ _____ .

   a. lost cause
   b. last straw
   c. hot air

2. It feels good to relax after you accomplish some necessary _____ .

   a. eager beavers
   b. odds and ends
   c. part and parcel

3. Having _____ with him is no fun because his mouth never stops moving!

   a. small talk
   b. ups and downs
   c. hot air

4. Because his mouth never stops moving, most of what he says is a lot of _____ .

    a. small talk
    b. ups and downs
    c. hot air

5. Most of the _____ in this country do not work very seriously or productively.

    a. old hand
    b. rank and file
    c. eager beavers

6. The criminal was ignored completely by his own _____ .

    a. big shot
    b. flesh and blood
    c. old hand

7. When I make a final decision, I never have any _____ .

    a. close calls
    b. pins and needles
    c. second thoughts

8. When it's a matter of _____ , I'm usually the one who has to compromise.

    a. ins and outs
    b. give and take
    c. white lie

VI. WRITING EXERCISE

Please answer each question or statement by using each idiom in a meaningful, grammatical sentence.

1. If you had some small troubles on a car trip, what would be the last straw?

2. What was the last close call that you had?

3. Why do some people think that politicians are full of hot air?

4. How could a big shot become a "small fry" (an unimportant person)?

5. Have you ever told a white lie to anyone? Why or why not?

6. When did you have second thoughts about something?

7. Are you an old hand at anything? What?

8. Why do eager beavers annoy lazy workers?

9. When, if ever, do you enjoy small talk?

10. Do you think that the world situation is a lost cause? Why or why not? (You might want to write a small paragraph on this topic.)

14

Adjectival Forms:
Pairs of Adjectives

cut and dried   spick-and-span
fair and square   short and sweet
few and far between   neck and neck
free and easy   up and about
null and void   touch and go

I. GUESSING THE MEANING FROM CONTEXT

Guess the meaning of each idiom as it is used in the following sentences. Provide either a synonym or a definition. Underline the context clues which help you to guess the meaning.

1. Tom had seen the movie three times before, so the outcome was rather **cut and dried** the fourth time. _____

2. In the difficult court case, the judge's decision was **fair and square** for both sides. _____

3. It takes me a long time to save enough money for a nice vacation, so such trips are **few and far between** for me. _____

4. Workers who are not at all eager beavers have a work attitude which is **free and easy.** _____

5. When the Immigration Service learned that George's wife was not a U.S. citizen, it declared the marriage **null and void.** _____

6. The maid took a long time to make the dirty kitchen **spick-and-span.** _____

7. The politician's speech was surprisingly **short and sweet;** it only lasted ten minutes. _____

8. Three of the race horses were **neck and neck** all the way to the finish line. _____

9. The 40-mile swim put a lot of wear and tear on the swimmer's body, but after a day's rest she was **up and about** as usual. _____

10. The heart operation was so difficult that most of the time it was **touch and go**. _____

Class discussion:

Decide which idioms were easy to guess and which were not. Consider the importance of context clues in your decisions.

II. DEFINITION CORRESPONDENCE

Using **Exercise I** to help you, check your guesses by choosing the correct idiom which corresponds to the definition you see on the left side. Be sure to use context clues and to use the correct grammar forms.

cut and dried   spick-and-span
fair and square   short and sweet
few and far between   neck and neck
free and easy   up and about
null and void   touch and go

(without delay)   1. The chess game was _____ because the champion beat the challenger easily.

(in good health) 2. I hope that he's _____ quickly after his serious illness ends.

(illegal)   3. Although the President made his own decision, the Supreme Court declared it _____ and said that Congress had to decide.

(honest)   4. Although I would have preferred to tell a white lie, my answer to her was very _____ .

(boring)   5. I dislike any activity which is _____ because I prefer to be on pins and needles.

(uncertain)   6. The weather kept changing so our weekend plans were _____ until Saturday morning.

(very clean)   7. The Health Department expects every public restaurant to

be _____ .

(close together)   8. The two best runners in the track meet were _____

_____ for most of the race.

(unworried)   9. Young people tend to have a more _____ atti-

tude towards life than older people.

(infrequent)   10. The office worker hardly made enough money to buy gro-

ceries, so his visits to restaurants were _____ .

III. EXPLANATION OF THE IDIOMS

1. **cut and dried**—obvious, routine, straightforward

   The idiom is composed of two past participle forms, and is usually preceded by the verb *be, seem,* or *appear;* it can also be preceded by *make* and an object.

   My weekend of steady work in the yard of my house was rather **cut and dried.**
   Many political elections seem rather **cut and dried** because most politicians are full of hot air.
   The repetitiveness of my job on the assembly line makes it very **cut and dried.**

2. **fair and square**—honest, straightforward

   This idiom is usually preceded by the verb *be,* and sometimes the verbs *seem* and *appear.*

   Joe is **fair and square** with all his friends because fairness is part and parcel of his personality.
   Now that I am older, my parents' decisions appear more **fair and square** than they did before.
   The new contract settlement seemed **fair and square** to the rank and file in the factory.

3. **few and far between**—rare, infrequent

   This idiom is also used most commonly with *be, seem,* and *appear,* which always occur in the plural form.

   Fortunately, attempts to kill U.S. Presidents are **few and far between.**

If ups and downs in your life seem **few and far between,** then you are a lucky person.

4. **free and easy**—unworried, carefree

   Besides being used with the three common verbs mentioned above, this idiom can also precede a noun form, and in this case hyphens (-) are used.

   If young people seem **free and easy** with their money, it's because they have a **free-and-easy** attitude towards life.
   Playboys and the very rich tend to be **free and easy** about everything.

5. **null and void**—illegal, invalid

   This idiom is used with the three common verbs mentioned with the verb *declare* and an object. It always refers to some official action or decision.

   If teenagers get married without parental consent, their marriage is probably **null and void.**
   The appeal court declared the lower court's decision **null and void.**

6. **spick-and-span**—very clean, very neat

   This idiom is used with the three common verbs mentioned above and can also occur with *make* and an object. It refers to the cleanliness of places, not people.

   The hospital operating room always has to be **spick-and-span.**
   The restaurant appeared **spick-and-span** through the window, but some corners were quite dirty.
   The maid was an old hand at making the house **spick-and-span** quickly.

7. **short and sweet**—without delay, brief

   This idiom can be used with *be,* or *make* and an object. The word *sweet* in this idiom suggests that the shortness is preferred by someone.

   I was quite relieved that the politician's speech was **short and sweet,** and not full of hot air.
   The students appreciated the fact that the teacher made the exam **short and sweet.**

8. **neck and neck**—close together, even (in a race)

   This idiom can be used with the three common verbs, *be, seem,* and *appear.* The appropriate context would be some kind of race between people, animals, or sometimes vehicles.

The two long-distance runners were **neck and neck** in the last part of the marathon.

The two race boats seemed **neck and neck** as they rounded the final curve.

The three lions were **neck and neck** as they chased after the faster animal.

9. **up and about**—in good health; active after an illness

This idiom is used only with the verb *be*. It refers to the ability to move around after being limited by illness or injury.

It feels good to be **up and about** after a week of being indoors with the flu.

The heart operation restricted him to the hospital for several weeks, but now he's **up and about** and as active as ever.

10. **touch and go**—risky, uncertain

This idiom is used most often with *be*. It is used when the result or outcome of a situation cannot be predicted until the very end, and when a change in the situation could occur at any time.

The peace negotiations between the two warring countries were **touch and go** until both sides were satisfied with the give and take.

The results of the important election were **touch and go** until the last votes were in and counted.

The serious operation was **touch and go** as new complications arose and were solved.

Class discussion:

Now that you have learned the meanings of the idioms and how to use them in sentences, go back to **Exercise I** and **Exercise II** and check your answers. As you do this, consider the following questions:

1. How many idioms did you guess correctly in **Exercise I**?

2. How much better did you do in **Exercise II**?

3. Are there any idiom meanings which are still not clear to you?

4. Is there anything you have noticed about the grammatical usage of these idioms?

IV. LEARNING THE GRAMMAR RULES

Part A The adjectival idioms in this chapter are formed from different parts of grammar, such as prepositions, verbs, nouns, and real adjectives.

Examples:

The judge's decision was quite <u>fair and square</u>. (adjectives)
The heart operation was <u>touch and go</u>. (verbs)
The race was <u>neck and neck</u> all the way. (nouns)
Mary will be <u>up and about</u> in two weeks. (prepositions)

1. What word is used to join the two parts of each idiom? Do you think that another word could be used?

2. Which verb is most often used with these adjectival idioms?

Part B Look at the following sets of sentences. Some sentences are correct and some are incorrect (*). Answer the questions by comparing the sentences.

Set 1

1. The judge's decision was quite fair and square.
2. *The judge's decision was quite fair or square.
3. The lecturer's speech was short and sweet.
4. *The lecturer's speech was sweet and short.
5. The hotel's kitchen was very spick-and-span.

a. How does sentence #2 differ from #1?

b. How does sentence #4 differ from #3?

c. What makes the idiom **spick-and-span** different from the other idioms in this chapter?

With these idioms, the pair of forms can only be joined by the conjunction *and*. In addition, the order of the forms is fixed. The two words *cannot* change position in any way.

The judge's decision was quite *fair and* (correct conjunction)
 square.

The judge's decision was quite *fair or* (wrong conjunction)
square.
The lecturer's speech was *short and sweet.* (correct order)
*The lecturer's speech was *sweet and short.* (incorrect order)

Set 2

1. Our vacations were few and far between.
2. *We had few-and-far-betwèen vacations.
3. Joe's attitude towards work was free and easy.
4. Joe had a free-and-easy attitude towards work.

a. How has the idiom in sentence #1 changed in #2?

b. What is the difference between the two idioms in the sentences above?

With some idioms in this lesson, the adjective form may be placed before the noun if hyphens (-) are used; in other cases, this is not possible.

Regardless of whether the idioms were formed from verbs, prepositions, nouns, or real adjectives, the pairs of forms are considered to be real *adjective forms.* This is one reason why they are called idioms.

V. MULTIPLE-CHOICE EXERCISE

Choose the idiom from this chapter, or the previous two chapters, which has the best meaning in the context below. No idiom is used twice as a correct answer. Be careful about the grammar rules which you have learned.

1. Students usually dislike homework because often it's simply

   too _____ .

   a. pins and needles
   b. last straw
   c. cut and dried

2. If you're too _____ with your money now,

   you'll have nothing saved for your old age.

   a. big shot
   b. free and easy
   c. spick-and-span

3. If you tell too many _____ , it will become a

   habit, and no one will ever believe you.

   a. white lies
   b. second thoughts
   c. fair and square

4. The _____ on my car makes it necessary for

   me to sell it very cheaply.

   a. close call
   b. ups and downs
   c. wear and tear

5. I hope that the teacher doesn't declare my test _____

   _____ because I cheated.

   a. hot air
   b. null and void
   c. last straw

6. A free-and-easy worker can never be an _____ .

   a. old hand
   b. eager beaver
   c. ins and outs

7. The close soccer game was _____ until thirty

   seconds before the end of the game.

   a. touch and go
   b. give and take
   c. neck or neck

8. John enjoys serious discussion more than _____

   _____ .

   a. heart and soul
   b. small talk
   c. hots airs

9. It was amazing that she was _____ so soon after

   her accident.

   a. lost cause
   b. up and about
   c. spick-and-span

10. It was the _____ when my neighbor played his

    stereo very loud for the fourth night in a row.

    a. part and parcel
    b. ups and downs
    c. last straw

VI. WRITING EXERCISE

Please answer each question by using the idiom in a meaningful, grammatical sentence.

1. What kinds of books do you usually find cut and dried?

2. Why should a judge be fair and square in his decisions?

3. Which of your activities are few and far between?

4. Do you put your heart and soul into your work or are you free and easy about it? Why?

5. Why are some old laws declared null and void as time passes?

6. Is your house or apartment spick-and-span or is it in average condition?

7. Why do people prefer speeches that are short and sweet?

8. Why are races more interesting if some racers are neck and neck?

9. Would you prefer to be resting in bed or would you prefer to be up and about? Why?

10. When could an international crisis be touch and go?

15

Adjectival Forms:
Various Compounds

clear-cut   man-to-man
easy-going   narrow-minded
all-out   first-rate
half-hearted   stuck-up
level-headed   close-mouthed

I. GUESSING THE MEANING FROM CONTEXT

Guess the meaning of each idiom as it is used in the following sentences. Provide either a synonym or a definition. Underline the context clues which help you to guess the meaning.

1. To me, the points in his lecture were **clear-cut;** he was not just full of hot air.

2. A person who is free and easy in attitude also is generally **easy-going** in behavior.

3. When someone puts his heart and soul into his work, he makes an **all-out** effort to do the best possible job.

4. On the other hand, a free and easy person will only make a **half-hearted** effort to do the minimum required.

5. The policeman managed to stay **level-headed** in the confrontation with the armed bank robbers.

6. I don't believe in telling white lies, so I had a **man-to-man** talk with Joe about our problem.

7. A big shot often thinks he knows everything, and is, therefore, frequently **narrow-minded** about accepting the opinions of others.

8. The dinner we had at the expensive restaurant was **first-rate;** everything was delicious and served perfectly hot.

9. After the handsome student became a football star, he be- _____ came very **stuck-up** and wouldn't have small talk with any of his old friends.

10. Tom had second thoughts about sharing his problem with _____ his family, so he decided to remain **close-mouthed** about it.

Class discussion:

Decide which idioms were easy to guess and which were not. Consider the importance of context clues in your decisions.

II. DEFINITION CORRESPONDENCE

Using **Exercise I** to help you, check your guesses by choosing the correct idiom which corresponds to the definition you see on the left side. Be sure to use context clues and to use the correct grammar forms.

clear-cut	man-to-man
easy-going	narrow-minded
all-out	first-rate
half-hearted	stuck-up
level-headed	close-mouthed

(excellent)   1. John really enjoyed the _____ movie starring

two of his favorite actors.

(sensible)   2. Even though most passengers were on pins and needles

about the engine problem, the pilot remained very

_____ .

(secretive)   3. Jim was _____ about his arrest because he

didn't want others to know about it.

(clearly stated)   4. The committee chairman thought that the plans were _____

_____ and that everyone knew what do.

(prejudiced)   5. When a person enters another country and culture for a

period of time, he must be careful not to be _____

_____ about new customs.

(unhurried)   6. It is often said that people who are _____

about their lives will live longer than nervous, busy people.

(uninterested)   7. Several members of the group made only a _____

_____ effort to help out on the picnic.

(snobbish)   8. Children of very wealthy, upper-class parents are often

_____ in school with other children.

(complete)   9. An eager beaver will always go _____ to please

his boss in every way.

(sincere)   10. A father and son who share many experiences together are

more likely to have _____ discussions.

III. EXPLANATION OF THE IDIOMS

1. **clear-cut**—clearly stated; definite

   This idiom is usually used with the three typical verbs *be, seem,* and *appear.* It may also precede nouns such as *position, stand,* and *explanation.*

   The lecturer's presentation was **clear-cut** and enjoyable.
   The lawyer gave a **clear-cut** explanation of his arguments to the judge.
   Our position seems **clear-cut**: we have to reduce wasteful spending and increase productivity.

2. **easy-going**—unhurried, relaxed

   This idiom occurs with the three typical verbs listed above and can precede nouns such as *attitude* and *approach.*

   Your new roommate seems **easy-going** and fun to be with.
   Tom's **easy-going** attitude made it difficult to get him to work hard.
   If you have an **easy-going** approach towards life, you'll survive the ups and downs more easily.

3. **all-out**—complete, thorough, out-and-out

   This idiom sometimes is used with the verb *be,* but often with the verb *go.* It also occurs with the verb *make* and precedes nouns such as *effort* and *attempt.*

The advertising campaign for the new product was **all-out** in hopes of attracting consumers.

We made an **all-out** effort to save the burning house, but failed.

We went **all-out** to salvage the sinking boat, but it was a lost cause.

4. **half-hearted**—uninterested, unenthusiastic

The three typical verbs, *be, seem,* and *appear* are used with this adjective. It may also occur with the verb *make* and precede noun forms such as *effort* and *attempt.* The meaning suggests that someone is not interested in doing something, for some personal reason.

Joe seems **half-hearted** about spending his weekend helping us to move, and I imagine he'll refuse.

Tom, at least, made a **half-hearted** attempt to offer some help, but never went all-out.

If his attitude is **half-hearted,** it's because his heart and soul are not in our project.

5. **level-headed**—sensible, practical

The three typical verbs, *be, seem,* and *appear* are used, and idiom also occurs following the verbs *stay* and *remain.* The common context is a situation of serious danger or threat.

Tom often seems on pins and needles; is he really **level-headed?**

Joe seems very **level-headed** for a young adult in such a difficult, demanding job.

The doctor remained **level-headed** when his touch-and-go operation suddenly worsened.

6. **man-to-man**—sincere, direct; heart-to-heart

The verb *be* is rarely used with this idiom. It is most likely used before nouns such as *talk* and *discussion.* When applied to women, *heart-to-heart* is used most frequently and carries the same meaning.

Instead of our usual small talk, we had a **man-to-man** discussion about our marital problems.

Joan had a **heart-to-heart** talk with her mother about sex.

Let's have a **man-to-man** talk about our financial problems.

7. **narrow-minded**—prejudiced; limited, short-sighted

The three typical verbs are usually used, and the idiom can precede nouns such as *attitude* and *opinion.* The meaning suggests that someone dislikes or hates other people or their beliefs, or is so limited in his thinking that other people's thoughts are never considered seriously. The opposite meaning is *broad-minded*.

We can say that people who discriminate against minorities are very **narrow-minded.**

You would be **narrow-minded** if you thought that the problem was so cut and dried; in reality, it is much more complicated.

People who have **narrow-minded** attitudes generally are not fair and square towards others.

8. **first-rate**—excellent, superior, of best quality

This idiom usually occurs with *be* and may precede noun forms of various kinds.

That exciting movie certainly was **first-rate!**

David thought his meal was **first-rate,** but Mary thought hers was only second-rate.

In my opinion, Switzerland has some **first-rate** mountain scenery.

9. **stuck-up**—snobbish, conceited; selfish

The three typical verbs, *be, seem,* and *appear* are used, and the idiom may precede nouns such as *attitude* and *personality*. The meaning suggests that someone thinks that he is above, or better than, others.

Why is the football star too **stuck-up** to talk with me?

Famous young actors and actresses often have **stuck-up** personalities.

10. **close-mouthed**—uncommunicative; secretive

This idiom is used with the verbs *remain* and *stay,* in addition to the three typical verbs above.

Some people are basically **close-mouthed** about their personal feelings and opinions.

Jane remained **close-mouthed** about her dismissal from work.

Class discussion:

Now that you have learned the meanings of the idioms and how to use them in sentences, go back to **Exercise I** and **Exercise II** and check your answers. As you do this, consider the following questions:

1. How many idioms did you guess correctly in **Exercise I?**

2. How much better did you do in **Exercise II?**

3. Are there any idiom meanings which are still not clear to you?

4. Is there anything you have noticed about the grammatical usage of these idioms?

IV. LEARNING THE GRAMMAR RULES

Part A The adjectival idioms in this chapter are compound forms because hyphens (-) are used to join the parts of the idioms.

Example:

Jim is quite level-headed.
adjective

Most of the important grammar information for these idioms was provided in the detailed **Explanation.** To review, the basic facts are:

1. The three most typical verbs which can be used with these idioms are *be, seem,* and *appear.*
2. In most cases the adjectives can also occur before a noun form.
3. Some of the idioms also occur after the verb *make* + object, while others can be used after *stay, remain,* or *go.*

Part B Look at the following sets of sentences. Some sentences are correct and some are incorrect (*). Answer the questions by comparing the sentences.

Set 1

1. Jill is quite level-headed.
2. *Jill is quite headed-level.
3. Tom and Jerry had a man-to-man talk.
4. *Tom and Jerry had a men-to-men talk.

a. What is the difference between sentences #1 and #2?

b. How does sentence #4 differ from #3?

c. Circle the correct answer:

The idioms in this lesson (can or cannot) change in form.

Although the idioms are made from different parts of grammar, as adjectives they cannot be changed in any way.

Jill is quite *level-headed*.   (correct order)
*Jill is quite *headed-level*.   (incorrect order)
Tom and Jerry had a *man-to-man* talk.   (correct singular form)
*Tom and Jerry had a *men-to-men* talk.   (incorrect plural form)

Set 2

1. Jill is quite level-headed.
2. Jill has a level head.
3. Are you half-hearted about helping others?
4. *Do you have a half heart about helping others?

a. How does sentence #2 differ from #1?

b. How does sentence #4 differ from #3?

c. How does the idiom **half-hearted** differ from the idiom **level-headed?**

Some of the adjectival idioms are formed from adjective + noun combinations; others were not formed in this way.

Jill is quite *level-headed*.   (compound adjective)
Jill has a *level head*.   (adjective + noun)
Jane was *close-mouthed* about it.   (compound adjective)
Jane kept a *closed mouth* about it.   (adjective + noun)
Are you rather *half-hearted* about   (compound adjective)
  working?
*Do you have a *half heart* about   (adjective + noun form
  working?   is incorrect)

There are no easy ways to remember this information; you have to review and practice the forms until you have learned the important information thoroughly.

V. MULTIPLE-CHOICE EXERCISE

Choose the idiom from this chapter, or the previous three chapters, which has the best meaning in the context below. No idiom is used twice as a correct answer. Be careful about the grammar rules which you have learned.

1. He went _____ to put his heart and soul into it.
   a. neck and neck
   b. first-rate
   c. all-out

2. Unfortunately, our serious discussion turned into uninteresting _____ .
   a. second thoughts
   b. hot air
   c. small talk

3. Even though he's rather _____ , he's not at all free and easy with his money.
   a. easy-going
   b. level-headed
   c. stuck-up

4. Studying hard should be _____ of every serious student's life.
   a. half-hearted
   b. part and parcel
   c. ins and outs

5. From his clear-cut answers, I can tell the professor is an _____ at responding to questions from his students.
   a. eager beaver
   b. ins and outs
   c. old hand

6. Because the rain destroyed her weekend plans, Miss Jones half-heartedly did some _____ around the house.
   a. wear and tear
   b. odds and ends
   c. give and take

7. How soon will Doug be _____ after the operation on Tuesday?
   a. null and void
   b. up and about
   c. spick-and-span

8. On Thanksgiving, all my _____ gathered at my house for a big family dinner.
   a. big shots
   b. flesh and blood
   c. last straw

9. The international nuclear crisis was _____ until the very end.
   a. touch and go
   b. clear-cut
   c. null and void

10. That speeding motorist almost didn't see me; that was a _____ .
    a. pins and needles
    b. close call
    c. lost cause

VI. WRITING EXERCISE

Please answer each question by using the idiom in a meaningful, grammatical sentence.

1. Why should a teacher's explanation be clear-cut?

2. Do you prefer active, energetic people or more easy-going, relaxed people? Why?

3. When should you make an all-out effort to help someone?

4. When do you feel half-hearted about work?

5. In a dangerous situation, why is it better to remain level-headed?

6. When should a father have a man-to-man talk with his son?

7. Is it better to be narrow-minded or broad-minded? Why?

8. In what situation would you prefer to stay close-mouthed?

9. What are the first-rate universities in the U.S.?

10. Do you enjoy people who are stuck-up? Why or why not?

16

Various Adverbial Forms

time and again	little by little
day in and day out	all at once
now and again	sooner or later
for now	high and low
for good	by and large

I. GUESSING THE MEANING FROM CONTEXT

Guess the meaning of each idiom as it is used in the following sentences. Provide either a synonym or a definition. Underline the context clues which help you to guess the meaning.

1. Even though I've tried many times to repair my car, **time and again** it won't start.   _____

2. She never has time to take a vacation; she's busy with her work **day in and day out.**   _____

3. My old friend used to visit me **now and again** on some weekends, but lately her visits have been few and far between.   _____

4. **For now** we'll go to work by bus, but soon we'll have to buy a car for convenience.   _____

5. John finally was able to quit smoking **for good;** he'll never touch another cigarette.   _____

6. John hadn't been able to do it suddenly; he had to control his smoking desire **little by little.**   _____

7. On the other hand, some people are able to quit **all at once** and never consider the idea of smoking again.   _____

8. Although people would like to live forever, everyone has to die **sooner or later.**   _____

9. When I lost my keys, I had to look **high and low** before I finally found them.   _____

10. **By and large,** Tom is an easy-going person in almost everything he does.   _____

Class discussion:

Decide which idioms were easy to guess and which were not. Consider the importance of context clues in your decisions.

II. DEFINITION CORRESPONDENCE

Using **Exercise I** to help you, check your guesses by choosing the correct idiom which corresponds to the definition you see on the left side. Be sure to use context clues and to use the correct grammar forms.

time and again	little by little
day in and day out	all at once
now and again	sooner or later
for now	high and low
for good	by and large

(eventually)   1. David really doesn't want to make an all-out effort to find a

job, but _____ he knows that he'll have to.

(everywhere)   2. When the rainy season started, Mary had to look _____

_____ for her umbrella, which was hidden in the back of a

closet.

(permanently)   3. The famous actor thinks he's so great that he'll probably be

stuck-up _____ .

(daily)   4. I really dislike having to drive to work in the heavy rush-

hour traffic _____ .

(occasionally)   5. _____ I take the bus to work so that I don't

have to worry about the traffic, but it takes longer!

(suddenly)   6. The sun was shining just a few minutes ago, but _____

_____ a bad storm came into the area.

(generally)   7. _____ , you'll live longer if you try to be more

easy-going about life.

(temporarily)   8. _____ I'll have to stay at home because of my

injured leg, but soon I'll be up and about as usual.

(repeatedly)   9. Some people are so full of hot air that they tell the same

ideas to the same people _____ .

(gradually)   10. The patient's serious condition was touch and go for quite a

while, but _____ it began to improve.

III. EXPLANATION OF THE IDIOMS

1. **time and again**—repeatedly

   Related forms: over and over; again and again

   Time and again he tried to act like a big shot, but each time
      we ignored him.
   Bill likes to tell white lies **time and again** as excuses for his
      mistakes.

2. **day in and day out**—daily, continuously

   Related forms: day after day; year in and year out (for
      longer periods)

   Housewives who have nothing else to do watch the same TV
      shows **day in and day out.**
   I dislike my neighbors because **day in and day out** they play
      their stereo loudly.

3. **now and again**—occasionally

   Related forms: on occasion; once in a while; from time to
      time; (every) now and then; every so often; off and on; at
      times
   Don't confuse this idiom with **time and again.**

   Now and again Larry and his wife go out to dinner at an ex-
      pensive, first-rate restaurant.
   It's nice for fathers to have man-to-man talks with their sons
      now and again.

4. **for now**—temporarily

   Related forms: at the moment; for the time being
   This idiom suggests that a change will occur some time soon.

   Although I have second thoughts about your plan, I'll accept it **for now.**
   For now we should assume that it's not a lost cause, but the situation easily might become worse.

5. **for good**—permanently, forever

   Related forms: once and for all; for keeps; from now on

   After the drunk driving arrest, Mr. Jones quit drinking **for good.**
   When Bill graduated from college, he was glad that his studies were finished **for good.**

6. **little by little**—gradually

   Related forms: by degrees; step by step

   Little by little, the foreign student improved his English abilities.
   Joe's love for his girlfriend continued to increase **little by little.**

7. **all at once**—suddenly

   Related forms: all of a sudden; in a flash

   All at once the soldiers attacked the enemy to surprise them.
   The audience in the theater laughed at the actor's mistake **all at once.**
   All at once the rainstorm turned into a snowstorm.

8. **sooner or later**—eventually

   Related forms: in the long run; in time; in due course

   Sooner or later all big shots lose their power and become small fries.
   Even if you are suffering ups and down, things will improve **sooner or later.**

9. **high and low**—everywhere

   Related forms: here and there; far and wide; far and near

   Jeff had to look **high and low** before he could find his old high school yearbook.
   The restaurant kitchen was so spick-and-span that the health inspector had to search **high and low** to find some dust.

10. **by and large**—generally

   Related forms: in general; as a rule; all in all; on the whole

   By and large, Americans are rather easy-going people.
   I don't like sour fruit like lemons **by and large.**
   By and large, Bill stays in bed late on the weekends.

Class discussion:

Now that you have learned the meanings of the idioms and how to use them in sentences, go back to **Exercise I** and **Exercise II** and check your answers. As you do this, consider the following questions:

1. How many idioms did you guess correctly in **Exercise I?**

2. How much better did you do in **Exercise II?**

3. Are there any idiom meanings which are still not clear to you?

4. Is there anything you have noticed about the grammatical usage of these idioms?

IV. LEARNING THE GRAMMAR RULES

Part A The adverbial idioms and related forms in this chapter are formed from various parts of grammar, such as nouns, adjectives, prepositions, and real adverbs. Although most use the conjunction *and,* other forms also occur.

Examples:

He makes the same mistake <u>time and again.</u>   (noun and adverb)

I go to work <u>day in and day out.</u>   (nouns and prepositions)

<u>Little by little</u> Tom's grades improved.   (adjectives and preposition)

<u>All at once</u> it started to rain.   (adjective, preposition, and adverb)

1. How do the first two sentences differ from the second two sentences?

2. Do you think that these idioms can be put anywhere else in the sentences?

Part B Look carefully at the following sets of sentences. Some sentences are correct and some are incorrect (*). Answer the questions by comparing the sentences.

Set 1

1. I like to go to the beach now and again.
2. *I like to go to the beach now or again.
3. Day in and day out, Bob stays at home.
4. *Day out and day in, Bob stays at home.

a. How do sentences #1 and #2 differ?

b. Where has the idiom been placed in sentence #3?

c. How does sentence #4 differ from #3?

As was the case with almost all the idioms in **Section II** of this book, the adverbial idioms cannot be changed in form in any way. This rule also applies to the related forms.

I like to go to the beach *now and again.*　(correct conjunction)
*I like to go to the beach *now or again.*　(incorrect conjunction)
Day in and day out, Bob stays at home.　(correct order)
**Day out and day in,* Bob stays at home.　(incorrect order)

Set 2

1. I like to go to the beach now and again.
2. *I like to go now and again to the beach.
3. Jim looked high and low for the book.
4. Jim looked for the book high and low.

a. In sentence #2, where has the idiom been placed? Where should it be placed?

b. How is the idiom **high and low** different from the other idioms in this chapter?

Because each adverbial idiom is composed of more than one word, it is almost never placed anywhere in the middle of a single sentence; the normal positions are either at the beginning or at the end of a sentence or clause.

I like to go to the beach *now and again.*　(correct position)
Now and again I like to go to the beach.　(correct position)
*I like to go *now and again* to the beach.　(incorrect position)

For now Tom wants to save his money.   (correct position)
*Tom wants to save *for now* his money.   (incorrect position)

The exception to the rule is the idiom **high and low,** as well as its related forms, which can occur in the middle of a sentence, after the verbs *search* and *look.*

Jim looked for his book *high and low.*   (correct position)
Jim searched *high and low* for his book.   (correct position)

V. MULTIPLE-CHOICE EXERCISE

Choose the idiom from this chapter, or the previous four chapters, which has the best meaning in the context below. No idiom is used twice as a correct answer. Be careful of the grammar rules which you have learned.

1. Ted is more than _____; he's basically just

   very lazy.

   a. narrow-minded
   b. easy-going
   c. easy and free

2. Wouldn't it be nice if we could eliminate all war and violence

   _____.

   a. for now
   b. for good
   c. time and again

3. _____, there are more similarities between

   various people of the world than there are differences.

   a. By and large
   b. Sooner or later
   c. Odds and ends

4. I'm surely glad that hurricanes and earthquakes are

   _____.

   a. high and low
   b. few and far between
   c. all at once

5. An eager beaver will work very hard _____.

   a. all-out
   b. day in and day out
   c. now and again

6. _____ must be part and parcel of all business

   and political negotiations.

   a. Give and take
   b. Pins and needles
   c. By and large

7. The judge declared the new law _____ because

   it was discriminatory.

   a. null and void
   b. all at once
   c. cut and dried

8. Little by little my car is receiving _____ because

   I drive it to work day in and day out.

   a. odds and ends
   b. lost cause
   c. wear and tear

9. Are you being _____ when you insist on such a

narrow-minded decision?

    a. last straw
    b. clear-cut
    c. fair and square

10. At first I accepted his suggestion, but later I had _____

_____ about it.

    a. second thoughts
    b. heart and soul
    c. small talk

VI. WRITING EXERCISE

Please answer each question by using the idiom in a meaningful, grammatical sentence.

1. Why is it necessary to study vocabulary time and again?

2. Why is it bad to work hard day in and day out?

3. What activity do you enjoy doing now and again?

4. What is your main goal in life for now?

5. What world problems should be eliminated for good?

6. Why are all languages changing little by little?

7. When might a person have to stop his car all at once?

8. What bad habit would you like to stop sooner or later?

9. Have you ever had to look high and low for something? Where did you find it?

10. By and large, what kinds of friends do you like to have?

Appendix

A. Explanation of Grammatical Terms

The following is a list of grammatical terms which are used in this book and other useful terms which instructor and student might want to use. This list should prove useful when answering the grammar questions and when talking about the grammar rules. Examples of the most important terms can be seen in the following section, "Outline of Grammatical Categories."

verb—a word which describes an action or state of being

transitive verb—a verb which is followed by an object

intransitive verb—a verb which is *not* followed by an object

particle—a word which is connected to the preceding verb in both meaning and grammar

preposition—a word which connects the verb and noun phrase which follows the preposition; the preposition is connected to the verb in meaning only and is connected to the noun phrase in grammar

subject—a noun phrase which is placed before a verb

object—a noun phrase which follows a verb

noun—a word which names something, such as a person, place, thing, or quality

pronoun—a noun substitute such as *he, she, it,* etc.

adjective—a word which modifies a noun

adverb—a word which modifies a verb, adjective, or another adverb

determiner—a special type of adjective which limits the noun that follows it; *articles* (a, an, the) and *demonstratives* (this, that, these, those) are the two kinds of determiners

noun phrase—a word or group of words which includes a noun or noun substitute (pronoun), and an adjective and determiner;

noun phrases are used as subjects and objects, and after prepositions

prepositional phrase—a phrase which consists of a preposition and noun phrase

B. Outline of Grammatical Categories

All of the grammatical categories, illustrative examples, and significant rules incorporated in the grammar part of each chapter are outlined below. They are intended as a handy reference for student and teacher alike.

Chapter 1 intransitive verb + particle

$$\underbrace{\text{A large carnation}}_{\text{subject}} \quad \underbrace{\text{stood out}}_{\text{verbal idiom}} \quad \underbrace{\text{on his suit.}}_{\text{prepositional phrase}}$$

1. Objects cannot follow intransitive forms.
2. No adverb can be placed between the verb and particle.

Chapter 2 intransitive verb + preposition

$$\underbrace{\text{The lecturer}}_{\text{subject}} \underbrace{\text{touched}}_{\text{verbal}}\overbrace{\underbrace{\text{on}}_{\text{idiom}}\text{many interesting ideas.}}^{\text{prepositional phrase}}$$

1. The prepositional phrase is a unit of grammar; the verbal idiom is a unit of special meaning.
2. Adverbs may be placed between the verb and preposition.

Chapter 3 intransitive verb + particle + preposition

$$\underbrace{\text{John}}_{\text{subject}} \underbrace{\text{came up}}_{\text{verbal}}\overbrace{\underbrace{\text{with}}_{\text{idiom}}\text{a fine solution.}}^{\text{prep. phrase}}$$

1. The verb, particle, and preposition are all connected in meaning.
2. The particle is connected to the verb in grammar and the preposition is connected to the noun phrase in grammar.

Chapter 4 Review

Chapter 5 transitive verb + movable particle

$$\underbrace{\text{The president}}_{\text{subject}} \quad \underbrace{\text{cleared up}}_{\text{verbal idiom}} \quad \underbrace{\text{the problem.}}_{\text{object}}$$

1. The particle may be placed on either side of the object.
2. An adverb may not be placed between the verb + particle or between the particle and object.
3. The rule for pronouns is that they always precede particles, but always follow prepositions.

Chapter 6   transitive verb + immovable particle (Type A)

My friends kicked my suggestion around.
subject — object (verbal idiom)

transitive verb + immovable particle (Type B)

Five rooms make up this house.
subject — verbal idiom — object

1. With Type A idioms, the particle may only be placed *after* the object.
2. With Type B idioms, the particle may only be placed *before* the object.

Chapter 7   transitive verb + preposition (Type I)

The executive devoted much time to her work.
subject — object — noun phrase (verbal idiom)

1. A preposition may not be placed before the object.
2. It is unusual for an adverb to precede the preposition because an object follows the verb.

Chapter 8   transitive verb + preposition (Type II)

The babysitter kept an eye on the child.
subject — object — noun phrase (verbal idiom)

1. Each idiom can only occur with one special object.
2. The noun form in the object cannot change in any way.

Chapter 9   transitive verb + preposition (Type III)

The instructor took my illness into account.
subject — verb — object — prep. phrase (verbal idiom)

1. Each idiom can only occur with one special noun in the noun phrase following the preposition.
2. The noun cannot change form in any way.

Chapter 10   transitive verb + particle + preposition

The participants got many ideas out of the conference.
 subject   object   noun phrase
          verbal idiom

1. The normal position for the object is before the particle, but with certain idioms the object may follow the particle.
2. A pronoun form will always be placed before the particle.

Chapter 11   Review

Chapter 12   nominal forms: pairs of nouns

Ups and downs are a part of life.   (prepositions)
The athlete put his heart and soul   (nouns)
   into it.
Marriage is a matter of give and   (verbs)
   take.

1. The pair of forms can only be joined by the conjunction *and*.
2. The order and form of the pair are fixed, and they are always used as nouns.

Chapter 13   nominal forms: adjective + noun combinations

White lies are never good.
There was a very close call!

1. Only one particular adjective can be used with any noun form.
2. The adjective cannot be deleted or altered in any way.

Chapter 14   adjectival forms: pairs of adjectives

The judge's decision was quite fair (adjectives)
   and square.
The heart operation was touch   (verbs)
   and go.
The race was neck and neck   (nouns)
   all the way.
Mary will be up and about in two   (prepositions)
   weeks.

1. The pair of forms can only be joined by the conjunction *and*.
2. The order of the forms is fixed, and they are always used as adjectives.

Chapter 15   adjective forms: various compounds

Jim is quite level-headed.

1. Hyphens (-) are used to join the parts of the idioms.
2. The adjective forms cannot be changed in any way.

Chapter 16 various adverbial forms

He makes the same mistake <u>time and again</u>.   (noun and adverb)

I go to work <u>day in and day out</u>.   (nouns and prepositions)

<u>Little by little</u> Tom's grades improved.   (adjectives and preposition)

<u>All at once</u> it started to rain.   (adjective, preposition, and adverb)

1. The adverbial forms cannot be changed in any way.
2. The normal positions are either at the beginning or at the end of a sentence or clause.

Index

leave to, 7
leave up to, 10
lend to, 7
let in on, 10
level-headed, 15
little by little, 16
live up to, 3
look back, 4
look back on, 3
look forward to, 3
look into, 4
look on, 1
look out, 4
look out for, 3
look up, 4, 5
look up to, 3
lose track of, 8
lost cause, 13

M

make a point of, 8
make light of, 8
make out, 5
make sense of, 8
make up, 5, 6
man-to-man, 15

N

narrow-minded, 15
neck and neck, 14
now and again, 16
null and void, 14

O

odds and ends, 12
old hand, 13
open up, 1

P

part and parcel, 12
part with, 2
pins and needles, 12
play by ear, 9
point out, 5
pull through, 7
pull to pieces, 9
put above, 7
put forth, 6
put off, 5
put through, 7
put to use, 9
put up with, 3

R

rank and file, 12
run across, 2
run around with, 3
run over, 2

S

second thoughts, 13
see off, 6
set aside, 11
set aside for, 10
settle down, 1
short and sweet, 14
show up, 1
small talk, 13
sooner or later, 16
spick-and-span, 14
stand out, 1
stand out from, 4
stick to, 2
stop over, 4
stuck-up, 15

T

take advantage of, 8
take after, 2
take a stand on, 8
take at one's word, 9
take charge of, 8
take exception to, 8
take into account, 9
take off, 5
take up, 6
take up with, 10
talk over, 5
talk over with, 10
tell apart, 6
think over, 5
tie down, 6
time and again, 16
touch and go, 14
touch on, 2
try for, 2
try out, 5
try out on, 11
turn into, 2
turn over, 11
turn over to, 10
turn to, 2

U

up and about, 14
ups and downs, 12

W

warm up, 4
wear and tear, 12
white lie, 13
work up to, 3